BIG
POTATO

To Mother –
Mary Magdalene Towers (Maggie) née Pywell
in fond memory.

BIG POTATO

A biography of
Joseph Austin Towers

Peter John Towers

BREWIN BOOKS

BREWIN BOOKS
56 Alcester Road,
Studley,
Warwickshire,
B80 7LG
www.brewinbooks.com

Published by Brewin Books 2018

A CIP catalogue record for this book is available from the
British Library.

ISBN: 978-1-85858-578-9

Printed and bound in Great Britain
by Hobbs the Printers Ltd.

Contents

Acknowledgements

My thanks to my brother Bernard for his three hour recording which kick-started this book. To Lucy who recorded the original chapters and to Jenny Upton who typed much of the later chapters and for her infinite patience as I changed things time and time again. Also to Sue for much of Dad's later life and to Mary Daniels who proof read and corrected my spelling and grammar.

Chapter 1

The Argument

The trouble with the Towers family was the stubborn streak that ran through the character of many of them. It was most evident in my father, Joseph Austin Towers and my grandfather, Joseph Towers.

The family had for many generations been involved in farming in the Erdington, New Oscott and Sutton Coldfield areas. In 1912 at the age of 21, my father was living at home on the Grove Farm, Erdington, working for his father where relations were often strained due to the stubborn streak already referred to. Grandfather would brook no argument and tended to rule the roost with a rod of iron. Father, now a grown man who had many arguments with his father over the years, was becoming increasingly unhappy by being denied any real input into the day-to-day decisions.

Grove Farm consisted of some 120 acres of arable and pastureland. The grass was used for beef fattening, sheep rearing and mainly a modest dairy herd with some cut for hay, which was used for winter fodder. The arable land was mixed with grain, potato and root crops. The climax between the two stubborn characters came to a head in 1914, when my father had been given the task of ploughing an eight-acre field in early spring.

The corn had been cut and carried the previous year, the field had been harrowed and lay dormant for the winter. With a spell of fine spring weather, good progress had been made with the single furrow plough, with three days seeing three-quarters of the task completed. Day four should complete the job as two acres a day was the 'going rate' for ploughing. Unfortunately all did not go well on the last day with one of the shire horses going lame. This necessitated a trip back to the farm with the lame animal, collecting a replacement from the meadow, re-harnessing and retracing one's steps – all in all a delay of the best part of an hour and a half.

The task could still have been completed by perhaps 7 p.m instead of the normal 5.30 p.m, but there was a complication. Father was due to call for Maggie Pywell at 7.30 p.m that evening and it was a question of getting back to the farm, seeing to the horses, getting a bite to eat, washing and shaving. Even then the task of harnessing up the pony and trap for transport to the Pywell Farm in Court Lane, Erdington had to be faced. As my father pondered all these eventualities and the prospect of facing my irate grandfather if the ploughing was not completed, the minutes ticked away as each furrow came to an end. Ploughing is very much a one-paced job with a pair of horses – it's not a question of opening the throttle and going a bit faster.

I'm pleased to say Maggie (my mother) won the battle. Father didn't finish the eight-acre field that night and he fulfilled his appointment with Maggie Pywell. Grandfather was out that evening, but in modern parlance the "balloon went up" over the breakfast table the following morning. Grandfather, verbally berated his son for not completing the task as instructed with all the old arguments about not having the interest of the farm at heart, ignoring instructions, letting private arrangements take precedence – nothing it seems changes over the years! Father on the other hand endeavoured to put his side of the story but to no avail. The final thrust came when grandfather said, "If you have no interest in the farm, you may as well clear off and I will find someone who will do the job!" The stubborn streak now surfaced in both and father told grandfather what he could do with the farm in no uncertain terms and that day he walked out of Grove Farm.

1. THE ARGUMENT

Perhaps the explanation as to why the relationship between my father and grandfather was not as cordial as might be expected between father and son goes back further. In 1869 Augustine Lewis Wells had married Eliza Clews at Maryvale Chapel and in early 1870 Elizabeth Wells was born. Through the later stages of the nineteenth century as Elizabeth and Grandad Towers, who were much the same age, approached adulthood, their paths would cross intermittently either at Mass on Sunday mornings, social occasions or agricultural shows. Throughout his teenage years grandad realised he was desperately in love and although Elizabeth was fully aware of his feelings, regrettably whilst she liked and respected him, courtship was out of the question. I suspect had the pendulum of fate not swung very much in grandad's favour, he would in all probabilities have remained a bachelor. There was no great pressure from the Wells family. Elizabeth would make her own decisions. Also there was a bit of a gap in social class. Grandad's family had always been tenant farmers, whilst the Wells family were substantial land owners.

As events turned out, and this is where grandad's prayers were answered, Elizabeth became pregnant. This was not exactly a novelty, attractive young girls throughout history have 'fallen by the wayside' and often solved the problem through abortion, adoption or accepting the child and the consequences. For the Wells family, strong Catholics, abortion was out of the question. The father was never named but rumour had it that a Catholic priest was involved and if that was the case marriage was certainly not an option.

Mr Wells was renowned for the work he did with local Councils. He was involved with the acquisition of Great Barr Hall by the Poor Law Authorities of Walsall and West Bromwich, and he was the Chairman of the first Committee. He was the first Chairman of the Perry Barr Urban District Council in 1894 and Chairman of West Bromwich Board of Guardians for two periods. He was on the Board of Wigmore School for twenty years, on the Handsworth School Board and a Governor for many years. All in all a reputation that would not be enhanced by a daughter fallen from grace. As Elizabeth wanted to keep the child, a long holiday and adoption was also out of the question. It seemed a natural solution, with Elizabeth's approval, that a quick marriage to Joseph Towers be arranged. Elizabeth demurely agreed, grandad was overjoyed and the union turned out to be a fruitful and happy one.

The Wedding ceremony took place on 24th March 1891 at St. Joseph's Catholic Church in Longacre, Aston, somewhat more discreet than in a blaze of publicity at Maryvale which was understandable in the circumstances. The officiating Priest was Father Chattaway. Joseph Towers (grandfather) was described as a Farmer of College Farm, Erdington, whilst Elizabeth's home was recorded as Warren Farm, Perry Barr. A comparatively small reception was held at Warren Farm.

Chapter 2

Reconciliation

Father had friends on the Chester Road, opposite Oscott College and this is where he took lodgings. Although he retained contact with his mother Elizabeth, sisters Freda, Muriel, Hilda, Biddie and brother Bernard, he always made sure his visits to Grove Farm were when his father was away. As grandfather had the tenancy of two other farms, one at Castle Bromwich and one in Sutton Coldfield, this was not too difficult to arrange.

Father had a little capital of his own and to make ends meet he purchased a carthorse and wagon and contracted his labour out to Sutton Council who were involved in road widening on the Chester Road. The horse and cart were stabled on a neighbouring farm to Grove Farm, which necessitated him passing his former home twice a day. On the odd occasion he passed his father no greetings were exchanged, the stubbornness of both still being very much in evidence.

Road widening in the early days of the twentieth century was very much a matter of pick and shovel – none of your modern earth moving equipment. Father always maintained he found it very difficult to slow himself down to the general level of work rate. He always reckoned he could manage four loads a day, moving the soil and rubbish from "A" to "B" in preparing the foundations for the widening of the road.

It appeared the going rate was either two or three loads maximum, so it was a question of slinging a shovelful onto the cart and then pausing for breath. The inference always was that he would be most unpopular with his colleagues if he showed them up. This story has to be taken with the inevitable pinch of salt, as it was not entirely unknown for him to exaggerate.

The situation prevailed for some six months. The relationship with Maggie Pywell blossomed and although forces within and outside the family campaigned persistently to both parties for reconciliation, neither would contemplate making the first move.

The catalyst for the eventual reunion came about with a most unique set of circumstances. The horse father had bought was a young, high-spirited animal and as already mentioned he had to pass Grove Farm twice a day. The entrance to the farm was up a drive and the boundary of the farm on Grove Lane was fenced for a short distance on both sides of the entrance by four feet high spiked iron railings.

On this particular day, he was returning from work to stable the horse and cart and passing the entrance to Grove Farm, when a corporation steam roller was rumbling along the road in the opposite direction, with father's horse becoming increasing agitated as the vehicle approached. Roads were not desperately wide in those days and as the steamroller drew level the horse panicked and shied away. Father jumped down from the cart with the intention of taking the horse by the head, but he was too late. The animal crossed the pavement, reared up and impaled himself on the iron railings. Pandemonium reigned and as fortune would have it, grandfather arrived on the scene. A vet was summoned, but there was no way to save the horse and it was put down on the spot.

Father was taken into Grove Farm and a horse was loaned to him to move his own cart, but grandfather insisted it was pulled into the Grove. With his mother also insisting he stayed for dinner and his father raising no objection, the rift was healed.

Subsequently, grandfather advised his son to sue the Corporation for the loss of the animal as he considered the steamroller was the cause of the accident and compensation was duly forthcoming, which at least meant he did not end up out of pocket. As subsequent events turned out, I sometimes wonder if this first brush with the courts and claim for compensation was the catalyst for future events with a much less successful outcome.

Chapter 3

Potted History

Joseph Austin Towers was born on the 28th October 1891, one of six children comprising two boys and four girls. He was born into a long established Catholic farming family with roots in the Midland area going back well into the eighteenth century. His father, Joseph Towers, while never a great land owner tenanted a number of farms, namely, Grove Farm of which mention has already been made and Langley Mill Farm, which now sits above the A38 Sutton Coldfield by-pass, and Hodge Hill Farm at Castle Bromwich, part of Lord Bradford's Estate. Lord Bradford was the resident at Castle Bromwich Hall prior to moving to Weston Park.

Other substantial Catholic farming families in the local area at that time were the Baines family, the Pywells, the Carrs, but none carried more weight or respect than the Wells family. It was indeed Elizabeth Mary Wells whom grandfather married and so united, at least in marriage, two substantial farming families.

After the family reconciliation, my father and Maggie Pywell married at Holy Trinity in Sutton Coldfield on the 3rd February 1913. They produced four children, the eldest being Bernard born in 1917, Tom followed in 1919, but he was never a robust lad. Doctors had warned my father and mother that a change for better or worse would probably occur at the age of seven and unfortunately the gloomiest of predictions was proved correct, with Tommy dying in 1926 at the age of seven. In his last few days, when asked if he would like anything, his request was for a puppy. A six-week-old mongrel was acquired and when asked to name her, Tommy whispered something like "Toosie". That was the name she was given – Tom died 48 hours later – and every dog we ever acquired in our household was forever called by that name. I should perhaps stress that every dog we had was a terrier mongrel cross, always a bitch as these were deemed to be far healthier, more robust, better ratters and being bitches, didn't stray so far. My sister, Patricia (Pat) was born in 1925, and perhaps this softened the blow of losing Tom, as far as my mother was concerned, and I, Peter, brought up the rear arriving in 1927.

Langley Mill Farm

After his wedding to Maggie Pywell, my father was offered the tenancy of Langley Mill Farm, consisting of some 100 acres of mixed arable and meadowland. Joe Towers had already had a good grounding in management of land and cattle, so he set out on his own farming career.

Inevitably the pattern followed much the same as at Grove Farm. Almost every farm had a cowshed where stalls enabled the cows to be milked. The stalls were either individual or more usually designed for two cows side by side. There was always adequate stabling for the numerous horses that were needed to keep the farm running smoothly. There would also be the usual farm buildings for storage and to cover machinery during the inactive winter months.

As at Grove Farm, father developed a dairy herd, some beef cattle for fattening, a few sheep and the usual cereals – mainly wheat and oats – and root crops, consisting of potatoes, swedes, turnip, mangoes and the like.

The farmhouse itself was a substantial building with spacious accommodation downstairs, four bedrooms on the first floor and a fifth bedroom on the second floor. The house was designed for servant accommodation with a main staircase serving the first floor and a second servant's staircase to the top floor. The substantial kitchen had the usual bells for summoning any staff to the various rooms.

Joe Towers, harvest time, Langley Mill Farm.

Joe and Maggie Towers with Bernard and Tommy, 1920.

Left and right: Tennis at Langley Mill Farm, c.1920.

Tennis at Langley Mill Farm, c.1920.

Tennis at Langley Mill Farm, c.1920.

Langley Mill Farm, Harvest Time, 1922.

Langley Mill Farm.

Tommy and Bernard, 1921.

As the family grew and the farm prospered, mother acquired a housekeeper/cook, and Bernard and Tommy in their young days had a governess to help with their early education, as Langley Mill Farm was way out in the country.

At this time, farming was a labour intensive industry, particularly at harvest times. Hay making, harvesting and crop gathering, always meant bringing in temporary workers and with an eye to economy, Joe Towers was never slow to seize every opportunity to cut costs. At that time in Erdington 'Highcroft Hall' was known as the local lunatic asylum. Some of the patients were kept in secure accommodation, but many were just mentally disturbed and no real danger to the general public. Even in those days it was recognised that some form of undemanding employment could be highly beneficial and as some farming tasks were not highly skilled, my father availed himself of some free labour from Highcroft when it suited his book.

Tragedy struck one day when one of the patients unfortunately cut his own throat in the darker recesses of one of the barns. One of the regular farm labourers found the poor man and ran to the farmhouse for help. A cursory examination from mother was of the opinion that there was not much hope for the poor wretch, but pony and trap were made ready to go to the nearest phone box to summon aid.

While all was panic and confusion, Bernard, then age five, decided he would go and have a look at this situation at first hand. Entering the barn, he could see nothing in the gloomy corners and had to feel his way. He eventually fell over the prostrate body and as the injured worker had not yet expired, he let out a strangulated 'Arrggh!' Up to the day he died at the age of 80, my brother swore he broke every sprint record in the book for a five year old, as he sought refuge back in the farmhouse.

Although the injured worker was taken to the Cottage Hospital in Sutton Coldfield, they were unable to save his life. In general, the authorities took the view that accidents like this were extremely unfortunate; the beneficial effects for the majority more than outweighed the odd disaster.

Langley Mill Farm, front view, 2017.

Langley Mill Farm, rear view, 2017.

The years passed at Langley Mill with the saddest year being 1926, when, as I have already mentioned, Tom died. There were many happy occasions, but already my father's Jekyll & Hyde character was beginning to surface. In a good mood he was charming company, a highly social animal and a good raconteur. Unfortunately, from mother's point of view, he was seen to have a weakness for a pretty face and a trim figure. This it seems was the basis for many of the arguments that developed between my parents and in his last three or four years at Langley Mill, Bernard sometimes sat at the top of the stairs listening to a blazing row going on below.

Chapter 4

Hodge Hill Farm

In the early 1920s, Birmingham was growing apace and farming land was being swallowed up fast to accommodate a growing population. In 1926, Grandfather Towers was notified that the Grove Farm was to be developed and he was given 12 months notice to quit. As he already had the tenancy of Langley Mill and Hodge Hill, he had no problem with an impending move and readers will see when I describe Hodge Hill, that it was inevitable grandfather would choose the former and my father would be redirected to the latter.

The move to Castle Bromwich took place in 1927 when I was a few months old, my sister two and my brother ten. I have already described Langley Mill with ample space, indoor sanitation and electric light. It must have been something of a culture shock to mother to be transplanted to a small semi-detached cottage with a living room, a small lounge, a scullery with a stone pantry. No bathroom, no indoor sanitation and no electricity. The privy was a combined building at the bottom of the garden shared by both cottages but fortunately with a separating wall some eight feet high, vision was restricted but sound was not! The wooden bench had the appropriate hole cut out and the metal receptacle below was emptied into the adjoining muck yard as and when necessary. Needless to say there was a chamber pot under every bed in the house for emergency purposes.

Hodge Hill Farm, Joe and Maggie with Bernard, Pat and Peter.

Hodge Hill Farm, harvesting potatoes, c.1932.

Hodge Hill Farm, Bernard in the muck yard, 1945.

Hodge Hill Farm, front view, 2017.

Hodge Hill Farm, rear view, 2017.

Hodge Hill Farm cottage on left, 2017.

The water requirements for the house were serviced from an old fashioned pump some 15/20 feet from the back door while the 'out house', a building adjoining the cottage, contained a substantial copper boiler serviced by its own fire below. On bath night, the boiler was filled by bucket from the pump, and some hours later, the tin bath would be placed in the living room in front of the fire and certainly Pat and I were given our weekly scrubbing. Bernard was, I assume, given the benefit of a separate bath as he was now a 'young man' and getting more and more involved in farming activities in his spare time. The bedroom facilities were equally sparse with my parents taking the main room, Pat and I sharing and Bernard taking the third bedroom.

The farm again was around 140 acres but this was spread around with some land on the Bradford Estate by Castle Bromwich Village and some fields beyond Hodge Hill Common. A substantial part of the farm was land within the triangle now formed by Bucklands End Lane, Hodge Hill Road, and Stechford Road. A small acreage comprising three fields was situated on the Fox and Goose side of Hodge Hill Common behind Ventnor Avenue, while 25 acres or thereabouts was cultivated on land now occupied by houses built in Eastbourne, Westbourne and Southbourne Avenues. About 30 acres was farmed on land rented from the Bradford Estate bordering Old Croft Road. Working a farm so diversified was a bit of a nightmare and it was natural that land well away from the farm itself was used for crops while that close to the farmhouse would be mostly meadow land to support the dairy herd and provide grazing for the various heavy horses which were essential as mechanisation was in its infancy.

Chapter 5

Milking

The operations at Hodge Hill Farm continued along much the same lines as at Langley Mill except for the fact that, as father was now that much closer to a residential area, it seemed a more profitable idea to sell one's milk production direct to the consumer, rather than to a larger distributor as at Langley Mill.

As with most farms the milking parlour, or cow shed as it was called in those days, was already in existence and the necessary cooling equipment was acquired. This was set up in the outhouse adjoining the cottage and consisted of a metal panel of connected hollow tubes through which cold water flowed from a tank situated above, which would have been previously filled. A further hopper alongside contained the milk brought straight from the cows, this would have been sieved to remove any hairs or flakes from the cows udder or teats although these would have been wiped before milking began. The teats would always be emptied by directing the first few squirts of milk away from the bucket, so that only the milk from the udder would go into the cooler and so on to the customer.

When the apparatus was turned on, the water flowed through the pipes cooling them down whilst the milk flowed over the outside thereby reducing the temperature before falling into a waiting churn. Milking took place twice a day at 6.00 to 7.30 a.m. and from 4.00 to 5.30 p.m. A cowman was employed and it was his job to complete the milking with limited help from Bernard and father if necessary.

As the milk yield from the dozen or so dairy cows varied according to their lactation period following calving, there were occasional periods when the milk supply fell whilst customers' requirements tended to remain fairly consistent. Father had a system where he would borrow from a neighbouring farmer, Joe Ryman, the odd gallon or so and repay when, following 2 or 3 cows calving close together, he would end up with a surplus. It was not entirely unknown, if desperate measures were needed, for the odd half bucket of water to be added to the churn, thereby creating a few extra pints. I feel reasonably safe in disclosing this bending of the rules as both father and my brother are now beyond the reach of any earthly law.

After milking, the cows would be turned out to grass in the summer or into the yard in the winter whilst the cowshed and stalls were swept and washed out and new bedding installed. All the waste matter, whether from the cowsheds, the stable or the pig sties, went into the muck yard for distribution onto the arable land before ploughing in the spring.

By the early 1930s, Bernard had left school and was made responsible for all the milking and as Hodge Hill developed with the private housing going up at a rapid rate, it was not only his task to milk, cool and bottle some of the milk, but to serve and develop the milk round. There was always a fair amount of competition for customers from the bigger distributors. The milk was served to customers every morning, the routine being milking and cooling 6-7.30 a.m. Breakfast for half an hour, then change into boots and leggings, harness up the pony and float, load the milk churns and bottles and away 8.30 to 9.00 a.m.

The pony knew the route just as well as Bernard and many of the customers would come to the float with a jug for their requirements, which were ladled out direct from the churns. If it was necessary for Bernard to take a few bottles to adjoining houses so that the pony and float had been left behind, a cry of "giddiup" would bring the pony along and a cry of "whoa" would bring him to a stop at the appropriate place. Something they haven't yet managed to do with the electric vehicles in this day and age, but with remote control no doubt it will one day, always assuming door to door delivery is not in its death throes!

As a very young lad when I accompanied my brother on his milk round at the weekend – father was never one to spurn the chance of free labour – it never ceased to amaze me how the pony, at what I suspect was the exact half way point, always quickened his pace so that as we turned into Bucklands End Lane some 400 yards from base, it was difficult to restrain him from breaking into a gallop. I believe the increase in the tempo was not entirely due to the lesser weight on board as the deliveries were made.

Somewhere around 1934, Bernard, who was by then 17 and with all the physical exercise that farming entailed, had developed a good physic and was quite a good looking lad. On one of his calls he was greeted at the door by an attractive, and by no means elderly, housewife who enquired if Bernard knew anything about dogs. As virtually every farm had a terrier or two for rat catching and perhaps a gun dog, we were no exception, so Bernard said he wasn't a vet but knew a bit about them. "Could you possibly have a look at my dog as he doesn't appear to be well and isn't eating?" Bernard's diagnosis was vague but he thought there was nothing to worry about. The following day he was met at the door again. It appeared the dog had slept upstairs and could Bernard possibly pop up and have another look. In his naivety, Bernard suggested she called the vet and excused himself. He related the story over the lunch table and was somewhat surprised later that afternoon to be told by his father to busy himself with another task after milking as father would do the milk round and er… "What was the number in Ventnor Avenue where the dog was not well?" As Bernard was back on duty the following morning, the charitable view is the dog really was off colour – the less charitable one – she preferred younger men.

Chapter 6

Haymaking and Harvesting

Haymaking and harvesting were two periods when most hours of daylight were used, providing there was not too much dew on the ground. Haymaking came first in early summer or thereabouts depending very much on Spring conditions and the rate the grass had grown. A dry day and indeed a dry field were necessary before the cutting machine could be used efficiently. This done, the cut grass was left in rows to dry in the sun before being turned so that the underside could also dry out and hay be made. From there comes the old adage – making hay while the sun shines.

One of the frustrations for the farmer in those days was a prolonged wet period setting in immediately after cutting and many is the time when the newly cut grass just rotted or became useless as hay. Other times the cut may be followed by a showery period so it then had to be turned so that the sun and air could dry it out. Even in my young days in the early 1930s, my sister and I would be delegated to join in with a pitchfork and turn the grass over as we walked along the row. It was a great relief when father acquired an appliance which, when drawn along the row by a horse, turned the grass over by a sideways facing wheel with metal prongs which skimmed the ground thus completing a row infinitely quicker than by hand.

Once the hay had been "made" the next task was collection and the building of the hayrick. The collection was made easier, again by 'modern' technology with the purchase of a horse pulled rake some eight feet wide. The prongs of the rake were curved so that a substantial amount of hay could be collected. This was then deposited by means of a pedal, near the seat where the operator sat, which lifted the prongs and dropped again when the pedal was released. Meanwhile a couple of workers would collect the hay with pitchforks from the newly established rows and load them onto the horse drawn cart where another worker would accept each forkful and carefully build a mini hayrick. Care had to be taken to make sure the load was safe for transportation with the four corners being carefully bound in with the following forkful, and as each tier was completed on the front, back and outside, so the middle was filled in to bind everything together. A substantial load certainly needed two good horses to pull it and sometimes in softer ground a third would be called for. Once back at the farm, the load would be taken straight into the rick yard where the haystack or hayrick would be built. This would take many loads and at around eight feet high, it would be sloped so that it had a pitched roof. This would then be thatched, so that it was protected from the rain and would be opened up in the winter months as fodder for the cattle and the horses when the grass no longer grew.

Some of the hay would be sold if there was a shortage elsewhere and in this case the hayrick was cut up into bales for distribution. All these tasks from the humble use of a pitchfork to loading the wagon, building the rick, thatching and cutting into bales are all tasks needing no little skill and a fair amount of physical strength: a far cry from the late twentieth century and the early twenty-first when silage and mechanical handling are predominant.

Personally, I still find the smell of new mown hay one of the most attractive in the old fashioned farming calendar.

With hay making out of the way, the next major task in the later summer was harvest time. This always came in school holidays and in later years, Pat and I had to make a contribution. When the signal came that the corn was ripe, the first task was to sharpen the blades on the "binder", this was the machine drawn by two horses which would cut and bind the corn into sheaves. Because the cutting platform was offset against the actual binder itself and the field to be cut had been sown up to the hedge, a path had to be cut so that horse and machine could make its first circuit. This would be done by hand with a scythe – a laborious job. I never became proficient with the scythe, but I had my share of gathering up the cut corn into sheaves and tying them with lengths of stalk so they could be gathered in due course. Not my favourite occupation. Once the headland had been cut, the binder blades sharpened and everything moveable had been oiled and greased, cutting could commence.

As the sheaves were thrown out, they were collected and put into stacks of anything between fours and tens with, obviously, their ears uppermost. There they would stay continuing the ripening process until the field was finished. Often Dad would invite either farming friends or any of his pals interested in shooting to come along for the last three or four hours. As the uncut portion of corn became smaller, rabbits would bolt and the strategically placed guns would certainly thin them out. I recall one occasion when I would be about six or seven, after a particularly heavy slaughter, I had difficulty getting to sleep. Mother, bless her, sensed the problem and sat with me until I dropped off.

As in hay making, the corn had to be collected, and again this was done by horse and cart. The same procedure was adopted with the sheaves being reasonably carefully handled, as the corn could be wasted if handled too aggressively. Again as each load was completed, it was ferried back to the farm where a rick was built and on completion, another would be started. I recall in 1934, after a particularly good hay making season and a fine harvest, there were some ten ricks completed, all immaculately thatched. The hayricks were tidied up by pulling out the loose stuff all round the four sides whilst those made of sheaves of corn were given a gentle trim on all sides. The finished effect really was very special and was recorded by a photograph which unfortunately has gone walkabouts.

At some later stage, usually the following spring or early summer, when the demand for the corn was strong, the threshing machine would be called for, and between the contractor and my father, a date would be arranged. This was always an exciting time as far as I was concerned, as the enormous machine was towed into the farm by a large steam engine. The thresher would be placed alongside the rick with the steam engine in front, the two connected by a driving band. Previously the rick would have had its thatch removed and a small fence of chicken wire built around the base of the rick.

It was a day's operation to put the sheaves through the threshing machine one at a time. The string binding each one had to be cut and each sheaf was carefully fed into the machine interior. With much shaking and vibrating, the corn was extracted and fed into a sack at one end, whilst the straw now only fit for bedding, came out the other end.

I was usually fortunate to have a day or so off school if it was not holiday time. The ricks had usually built up a healthy rat population during the winter months – not surprisingly as the thatch kept the rick dry and there was a ready supply of grain at hand to keep the greediest of rats content. As the sheaves were removed, nests would be revealed, rats would bolt, dogs would have a field day and any rats going over the side of the rick would be restricted to hiding in the rubbish at the bottom, only to be despatched later that evening when a general clearing up operation took place. In my tender years, I thought the whole operation was designed to exterminate the rat population and I must confess, I much enjoyed those days whether I was wielding a stick as a youngster or a pitchfork as I grew older and was able to make a working contribution.

In the winter months it was possible to walk round the rick yard and hear the vermin in the ricks and many the time my father and brother have emptied both barrels of a 12 bore shotgun into the rick in their frustration. Again the comparison with the modern combine harvester and new chemicals has improved the cleanliness and yield enormously, but one does not see the flocks of birds on newly harvested fields these days as were evident 30 to 40 years ago.

Chapter 7

Progression

As I grew up at Hodge Hill Farm, I look back and can hardly remember a single evening when my father stayed in. By the time I was four and my sister six, our brother Bernard at fourteen was now deemed to be a capable babysitter. Mother and father were keen card players and a weekly visit to the Folk House in Erdington became a must. The family had by this time acquired a square box like Rover and outings would take place at the weekends usually culminating on Hodge Hill Common with an ice cream purchased from a chap on a three wheel bicycle. Otherwise, in the evenings, father had a large circle of family friends and while we were at Hodge Hill Farm, the Coach and Horses at Castle Bromwich became his favourite watering hole, where George and Eunice Brown were mine host. They became firm friends of the family which was nurtured by the friendship of their daughter Brenda and my sister Pat in later years.

It was a couple of years after we moved to the farm in 1927, when my father was the proud possessor of a motor bike and sidecar that he chanced upon a stray remark over a pint at the Coach and Horses that really paved the way for him to enter the car owning democracy.

Part of the land, as I have previously mentioned, was spread around the Castle Bromwich area. However a good portion bordered the Eastern side of Bucklands End Lane up to Hodge Hill Common and along what is now Stechford Road as far as the pre-war development of Hodge Hill Road and down to the River Cole.

It appeared that Birmingham City Council had agreed with Lord Bradford that a strip of land which was part of the farm would be acquired for the development of housing facing Hodge Hill Common. This would take away approximately twenty acres of land for which a modest amount of compensation would come father's way. As the field had recently been harvested and was now lying fallow, no great sum could be expected. On hearing this on the Friday evening, arrangements were made to plough the field after a modest amount of manure had been scattered and a hardy strain of wheat was sown. The builder was not best pleased to have to raise his compensation payment but Joe Towers steadfastly maintained this was standard farming practice.

Worse was to follow from the builder's point of view. It was some months later that building commenced after a line across the fields for drainage into the River Cole had been agreed. Of necessity the drainage work was started first and after a couple of hours it was obvious that the builders were taking the wrong line across the fields. This was pointed out to my father by the Wagoner and I suppose most people's response would be to stop them and put them right. Joe Towers' reaction was to contact his old friend Bert Throup and suggest a trip to Norfolk for an overnight stay to review the agricultural scene in that county. This they did and on his return home forty-eight hours later he feigned, very realistically I'm told, substantial anger and outrage. He threatened to sue, was offered a couple of hundred pounds in compensation, said he would take three hundred whereby they accepted with alacrity. He subsequently always regretted his haste and wished he had asked for five hundred!

There was in fact a follow on from that development. Some years later when the housing development was complete, the rear garden obviously backed on to the reduced field and most residents had a hedge as a border. Quite a number had dogs as pets and although these would be exercised on the Common, if they were let out in the back garden one or two found their way through the hedge.

Peter Towers, aged 6, 1933.

There was no great problem until Joe Towers was approached by one Ernie Hunt with a scheme for selling pure bred fertilised chicken eggs. The going rate for these was 2/6 a dozen (12.5p) while general run-of-the-mill eggs fetched anything from 6 pence (2.5p) to 1 shilling (5p) a dozen. There was always fifty to one hundred chickens scratching around the farm to provide a ready supply of eggs for home consumption and the occasional sale. This project, however, called for more special measures.

Father had half of the field backing on to the new Stechford Road houses, wired off. The three acre section split into breeding areas. He then ordered ten hens plus a cockerel of various breeds including Wire Dots, Rhode Island Reds, Leghorns, Light Sussex and various other breeds, up to ten varieties. All were penned separately, eggs produced regularly and as the cocks were doing what cockerels do best, a profitable little side line was in operation.

Joe Towers had bought an incubator with him from Langley Mill and with surplus eggs the next stage was to hatch one's own and sell as day old chicks – another lucrative market. Things went so well, two further incubators were obtained and sales of day old chicks supplanted the sale of fertile eggs. That is until disaster struck. As I have mentioned most owners exercised their dogs on Hodge Hill Common, but when released into their back gardens, often found a gap in the hedge and stretched their legs in father's field. With the establishment of the chicken pens, this provided a lot of excitement for the dogs and animals got carried away. One dog broke into the enclosure and created mayhem. He must have had some fox blood in his veins for the destruction was wanton. One of the farm hands warned father about what was taking place and he wasted no time in despatching the animal with his twelve bore. The dog had a collar on with the number in Stechford Road so father presented himself post haste to inform them if they wanted the corpse they had better collect it and they would be hearing from his solicitors. The owners were mortified – it seemed the animal had appeared at Crufts was a thoroughbred and, like the cockerels he had despatched, had quite reasonable earning potential.

All in all the building of houses on the Stechford Road turned out to be substantially more profitable than the farming. As Bernard my brother always said, there was something fascinating about hatching eggs. The way eggs collected over a period of days, would all hatch within hours never ceased to amaze him. His keenness on poultry would land him in trouble at Home Farm Shenstone, however.

Most families have tragedies in their lifetime and I have already mentioned that mother and father had an early one with the loss of our brother Tommy at the age of seven. I do not think it is an exaggeration to say that either side of the First World War, farm workers were among the fittest in the land. An open air life and plenty of physical exercise was a good recipe for healthy lungs and a strong heart, so most accidents of whatever nature were perhaps unlucky. This was certainly so in 1936 when father's brother Bernard (my brother had been named after him) lost his life. Most farmers one hundred years ago were taught to ride at any early age. My father and Uncle Bernard were no exception and in their younger days they both hunted regularly, particularly in the Langley Mill days and this was often a meeting point for the local hunt. Mother would have the task of providing father and Uncle Bun with a flask and perhaps some toast to sustain them. Uncle Bernard took his riding very seriously and participated in many point to points and it was this passion that cost him his life. I remember father's sister Auntie Muriel and Uncle Frank coming to give us the bad news and poor Auntie Muriel was inconsolable. If there was a favourite in father's family I suspect it would have been Uncle Bernard. I reproduce a cutting from the *Birmingham Post* at that time which reported the unfortunate circumstances of the tragedy.

'A fatal accident to a rider marred the Wheatland Hunt P-to-P race at Haughton near Bridgnorth on Saturday 29th February 1936. The weather was atrocious, the incessant rain made the three mile course heavy and holding while the condition of the ground was such that the majority of cars were unable to enter the running field and had to park in adjacent fields and lanes, another disappointment was the absence of the Master (Miss Frances Pitt) who was unable to be present owing

Hodge Hill Farm, Bernard in the back garden.

Hodge Hill Farm, 1937. View from rear of gardens at Stetchford Road.

to illness. The fatal accident occurred in the fourth event the Farmers adjacent Hunts Race for maiden hunters and it concerned Mr Bernard Towers who was riding Mr G Wints horse "All Square". The incident occurred at the water jump three fences from the winning post. In some way Mr Towers was thrown onto his head and is understood to have received a fractured neck. He was taken by stretchers to an adjoining farmhouse. Mr Towers who was a haulage contractor residing at Bernards Hill, Bridgnorth and was recognised as one of the leading riders in the Wheatland Hunt. Until recently he conducted a riding school. He leaves a widow and family. "All Square" belongs to the well-known gentleman rider Mr G Wint who now lives in Bridgnorth, and but for being injured would have ridden the horse himself.'

Chapter 8

Home Farm, Footherley

As the country came out of recession in the early 1930s my father's thoughts turned to fresh pastures. Hodge Hill Farm was steadily being eroded as Birmingham required more land for expansion. The Glebe Farm Estate had been completed but as that was the other side of the River Cole it meant the loss of a few acres. There were outline plans for the development of the whole of the Bradford Estate but no one could really foresee in the mid-thirties that building would cease at the end of the decade as Britain entered the Second World War.

There was a second factor that necessitated a move. By 1936, I was nine, my sister eleven, and we were still sharing a double bed. As I have already recorded, Hodge Hill Farm's residential accommodation comprised two semi-detached cottages. We had three bedrooms, no indoor sanitation, chamber pots under the bed – all pretty primitive. After years with his own bedroom my brother was not going to have his young sibling moving in with him, so a four-bedroom residence became a must.

It was not difficult to find a farm to rent at that time and after an examination of various estates it became a choice between Shustoke in the Coleshill area or Footherley some five miles from Lichfield. I have often wondered what pattern the family's life may have taken had Shustoke been selected.

Anyway Home Farm Footherley was the choice and it was to there we headed in the summer of 1936.

The farm was part of a small estate comprising, I believe, three farms, Home Farm, New Barns Farm, some two miles nearer Stonnall, and a farm at Stonnall itself. Each farm was around one hundred and fifty acres in size within the Footherley estate, owned by Mr Ellison who lived at Footherley Hall. The Hall was some two hundred yards away from the Home Farm facing our land across the lane from the front and bordering meadow land from the side looking South East. It was agreed a certain amount of redecoration was necessary before we moved. My father still prone to exaggeration, maintained the decorators had to chip ten layers of wallpaper off the walls of the main lounge.

Anyway, the time came to move, Pat and I had not seen Home Farm before the move. You can imagine our excitement as the place was a veritable castle in comparison to Hodge Hill. Five bedrooms for a start, with a bathroom and an indoor toilet upstairs and downstairs. The ground floor was also immense in our young eyes. Entering through the front door, although, again like most farms everyone came round the back, a corridor ran down the middle with a lounge either side somewhere around eighteen feet by fourteen feet. Beyond the lounge on the right was an even bigger lounge of perhaps twenty feet by fourteen feet with a conservatory leading off. Beyond that was a large storeroom for bicycles, wellies, etc. and this led to the back door. On the left as one passed the lounge, a second corridor led to a stone pantry on the left and an office on the right. Between the office and main corridor was the kitchen cum dining room. Halfway up the stairs, they split left and right. To the left the main bedroom, my sister next to it, mine next to Pat's, my brothers to the right and a spare room to the right of that.

The farm itself consisted of one hundred and twenty acres of mixed arable and grass and a modest amount of woodland. On approach from the South, the farm is on the right of Footherley Lane and stretched as far as the railway line from Birmingham to Lichfield. On the other side of the lane a brook ran through a couple of meadows which were bordered by Footherley Hall and land belonging to New Barns Farm and an adjoining farm on the Birmingham side.

It goes without saying that there was a bit of a difference in running a house of this size compared with Hodge Hill and my father felt mother would need some domestic help. Whether my father's magnanimous gesture had any ulterior motive at that stage is a matter for conjecture. He had already met the Truelove family who lived in a modest single-story bungalow two hundred yards away and was employing a couple of the sons. There was a young daughter named Vera who was sixteen at the time and she was employed on a part-time basis to help in the house. Vera was a good-looking girl with a trim figure, a combination my father found very difficult to resist.

There had been stories of his philandering certainly at Hodge Hill Farm and even as far back as Langley Mill where it was suggested he had difficulty keeping his hands off the younger midwives who attended my mother during her confinement when pregnant with my sister and myself. At Castle Bromwich there were rumours of an affair with a local resident and my father certainly had plenty of opportunities, I have already mentioned he rarely stayed in at night.

So the employment of Vera was really like playing with high explosives. All was bearable for a year or so, although there was no doubt mother had her suspicions. It came to the point where she decided she could no longer tolerate Vera in the house and told her she was no longer wanted. This was not the recipe for domestic harmony and although I was not privy to the sequel, it was sufficiently vitriolic for mother to vacate the matrimonial bed and move in with my sister. Vera was immediately re-employed by my father to look after the chickens and if the hen houses could speak they would have a tale or two to tell. Certainly my brother Bernard, now aged twenty, often checked to collect the odd egg and see how the hens were doing. On one such visit he caught his father and Vera in a somewhat compromising situation and was told in no uncertain terms to forget what he had witnessed and to consider the hen houses off limits in future.

Chapter 9

Humdrum Days

Meanwhile farming activity continued normally. The dairy herd had been moved over from Hodge Hill but obviously the milk round had to be abandoned. It was sufficient now for the collected milk from the evening and morning milking to be placed in churns on a platform outside the gates to be collected by one of the major processors. I cannot remember ever seeing my father turn his cap back to front, settle on a three-legged milking stool and perform the necessary function. He had for many years operated under the dictum 'Why have a dog and bark yourself?' and had no intention of changing now.

One little anecdote re milking surprised my brother. As I entered double figures I had the odd cow to milk especially during school holidays and weekends. Some animals were extremely docile, others fidgeted and the odd one kicked. I had to milk a kicker one day and in a fit of petulance I whacked her with a stick that happened to be handy. I caught her on the protruding bone at her rear and she turned her head and gave me a hateful look. Talk about elephants never forgetting. She would always have a go at me if I ever got in range and my brother pooh-poohed the idea until we were in the meadow one day and I strayed a little way from him and near enough to this particular cow to give her the belief she could get at me. As she lumbered (charged would be an exaggeration) I fled to Bernard's protection. He merely waved his arms and the cow ambled off. He confessed he had never seen anything like it as I protested somewhat breathlessly 'I told you she didn't like me'.

I have in the past played dare devil games with this particular animal encouraging her to have a go at me, but only when I was certain I could out run her to the nearest wall or gate. The one task that filled me with trepidation was when my father told me to fetch the cows in for milking. This necessitated getting round the back of them and ushering them back to the farm. There was no real protection in this situation and I usually resorted to sending the dog (sheepdog fashion) to bring them in. Fortunately the cows knew when it was milking time and they didn't need a great deal of encouragement to head for the milking parlour.

The early year or so of my father's tenancy were spent getting what had been a neglected farm back into shape. Like many small farms at that time there was usually a spread of arable and grassland. The meadows were needed for the animals to graze and a certain acreage would be set aside if suitable to be cut for hay. The arable land was rotated for corn, normally oats, wheat or barley, potatoes or catch crops such as cabbage, sprouts, peas, carrots, etc. We had yet to enter the tractor owning fraternity and horses were still used for the hard work. Hoeing was one of the more boring jobs, whilst planting potatoes was perhaps slightly more interesting. This necessitated wearing a type of apron, made out of old potato sacks, having it filled with seed potatoes and then walking up and down the rows dropping a potato at the appropriate distance. The field would have been ploughed and ridged to provide a furrow to receive the potato and would subsequently be covered. As the crop sprouted, they would be earthed up to protect the young potatoes from the light.

Corn crops were sown by machine and needed perhaps less attention but the harvesting was very much the same as I have previously described, the only difference at Home Farm was the fact that there was now a substantial Dutch barn available. This took a large amount of the corn and hay thus eliminating the necessity for building the old fashioned rick.

As usual my father's participation in the running of the farm did not involve a great deal of physical effort. There would be the odd occasion when he felt an employee was not pulling his weight. In that case he would grab the pitchfork, hurl a few sheaves of corn for a minute or so at a pace no one could maintain for long, hand the fork back to the unfortunate worker with a suitable admonishment and amble off. Hard physical work needs to be undertaken in a controlled fashion with the occasional breather – a fact not always appreciated by Joe Towers.

Although my parents' marriage was by now obviously one that was not made in heaven, my father was never physically violent to mother. This did not necessarily apply to the animals or indeed to me. There was one occasion at harvest time when the corn was being collected. This was done by a couple of horses and presented no problem when the cart was empty. As it was loaded, it became more of an effort, particularly if the ground was a bit soft. One day, with the cart now fully loaded and ready to be taken back to the farm for storage, the team of two horses were somewhat reluctant to get it moving. The odd whack on the rump came to naught as father came across the field. The employees were castigated in no uncertain fashion as father grabbed one of the pitchforks and I can still see the look of apprehension in the horses' eyes as father "tickled" their bellies with the pointed end. The cart was on the move in seconds and once mobile could be kept going. The only snag from my father's point of view was that a couple of people witnessed the incident from the lane, reported it to the authorities and father was summoned to appear at the local court. He was reprimanded, fined a few pounds and told to treat his animals with more respect in future.

It was years before violence towards one's children was outlawed and I doubt that had it been in existence in around 1939/40 it would have saved me. Not that I suffered any lasting physical harm but my ego and social standing as the son of the farmer certainly suffered. It was at potato harvest time and for many years it had been the practice to employ women and their children in school holiday time to pick up the potatoes. As Home Farm was somewhat isolated, the potato pickers were collected by lorry for the day's work. The machine would be drawn along the furrow and it would throw out the potatoes which would then be collected. As soil had also been thrown out some potatoes would be hidden and my job was to drive the horse and harrow up the row to reveal any that were hidden. At the end of the day everyone made their way back to the farm and on this particular day I had not finished on the harrow. The worker, probably one of the Truelove boys, said 'did I want to drive the tractor back to the farm?' I readily accepted – a chance to impress the young girls who had come with their mothers. As I took control, he opened the throttle a little too vigorously and I was thrown a bit off balance. As I recovered and we were proceeding up the path at a fair rate of knots, I became aware that the harrow was on the path in front of me. The appliance is nothing more than an eight by four feet of metal spikes going into the ground. It would not have done the appliance any good had I gone straight over it but with what I still believe was a superb bit of driving I swerved to the left, missing a gate post by inches, straightened up and got through the open gate in front of the harrow, again without doing any damage. We were now in the meadow cum orchard heading back to the farm with most of the potato pickers also in the field. Unfortunately my father happened to be coming towards us and had witnessed the whole incident. I was ordered off the tractor and although I cannot recall the exact words of admonishment, I do indelibly recall having my ears soundly boxed in full view of all and sundry. Most of the workers the following day were sympathetic including the young girls and my image did not seem to have suffered too badly. I made a silent protest by not speaking to my father for a couple of days, but as I say it was my ego that suffered most.

Chapter 10

Family Life

With the move to Home Farm we, as a family, developed a social side that had not been evident at Hodge Hill. My brother, Bernard, would have his pals round to play cards but my parents would go to whist drives or the cinema. It was hardly conducive to entertain at Hodge Hill farm where there was no electric light and the privy thirty yards away at the end of the garden.

Now, however, Home Farm was a different kettle of fish. There was a substantial front garden and lawn and this was rapidly developed into a nine-hole putting green with the holes winding their way through and around the small flower beds set into the lawn. We seemed to have a one track mind with the summer planting, always geranium and lobelia. Golf balls, putters, cups and flags were bought and many happy hours were spent on sunny days honing one's skills. This was soon followed with the establishment of a grass tennis court on the left of the drive. The family had always been keen tennis players and my father now enjoyed having friends to visit. It was always his friends and his family never my mother's, although she was one of thirteen. Mother was the youngest of the first family of seven, her mother died shortly after her birth, grandfather soon marrying again and having a 'second' family of six. So mother was kept quite busy retaining contact with her own relations which usually meant visiting, thus presenting further opportunities for father's philandering.

The other form of entertainment was playing cards and this usually ended up with the gambling game of 'Farmers Glory'. This involved being dealt three cards and then you bet what you felt appropriate to beat the card the 'Banker' would turn up. If you held three high cards in a different suit, you could 'shoot' for the whole kitty. If you won you scooped the pool, if you lost, you doubled it. As children we were allowed to participate for a certain time and more often than not, we were allowed to come away with a shilling or two, by virtue of some over optimistic betting by parents and relatives.

So life was good for us children at least, although mother was not of the school where she could ignore father's infidelity. Rows were frequent but fortunately never violent. Father had a talent for grinding away. This could be avoided at home by mother moving away, but stuck in the car it was another matter. On more than one occasion, whilst travelling at 30/40 mph, mother had opened the car door and threatened to jump out if father did not relent from his diatribe.

Bernard also enjoyed having friends over to Home Farm, but as he had grown up from eleven to nineteen at Hodge Hill, many of his contacts were in that area. As a result he tended to gravitate back there for his entertainment, and among his many girlfriends was one Mary Ravenhall whom he met in the grounds of Castle Bromwich Hall. In an historical perspective with Grandma Towers (Elizabeth Wells) falling pregnant out of wedlock, and my father's inability to control his passions, it was perhaps no surprise that in the early summer of 1938 he managed to put Mary in the family way. Bernard was a grown man of twenty-one and, as will be revealed later, my father was in no position to be critical. But the announcement later in the summer did not go down well. I was not privy at that particular meeting but the announcement was not greeted with any great enthusiasm, based purely on the fact that Mary came from quite a modest family background. She was a good looking girl and like many youngsters over the years they both got carried away and perhaps thought it was long odds against them "hitting the jackpot". Joe Towers was farming well, making money and, although not a land owner, was beginning to think of himself as one of the gentry and Mary was, in his eyes, not in the same social class.

*Home Farm
working entrance,
2017.*

*Home Farm
rear view,
2017.*

*Home Farm
rear view,
2017.*

*Home Farm
Footherley,
2017.*

*Home Farm
front entrance,
2017.*

*Home Farm
main entrance,
2017.*

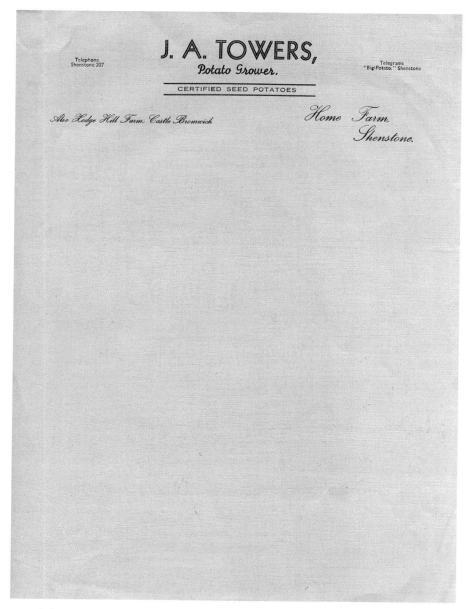

Headed notepaper.

It appears sleeping dogs were allowed to lie over the next nine months.

Maybe the Towers side had hopes of a miscarriage and therefore a release from any matrimonial obligations. It was not to be. Mary remained in vigorous good health and got bigger and bigger. Nothing seemed amiss in my young eyes in the Christmas of 1938 and unbeknown to Pat and I, Mary produced a bonny slightly ginger-haired boy on the 6th February 1939. I was vaguely surprised when I was told that my brother was getting married and duly attended their Wedding which was a very low key affair, at the Holy Cross Catholic Chapel in Lichfield on 23rd February 1939. In my ignorance, I saw nothing amiss when I was subsequently told that I was an Uncle at the age of 12. Such is youthful innocence. Bernard and Mary were fortunate that they were able to take up residence at Hodge Hill Farm thus commencing their married life with a water pump outside the back door, the privy down the garden, no indoor running water and a tin bath in front of the fire once a week. And Mary was supposed to be the lucky one!

Chapter 11

The Pinnacle

It was the winter of 1938/9 which saw my father's star in its ascendancy. It stayed there for a couple of years before catastrophe struck. For generations the Towers family had grown potatoes, and in the summer of 1938 he was not alone in growing a high yielding crop. There was one 10 acre field which had lain barren since we arrived in 1936. It adjoined the Lichfield/Birmingham railway line and was in places badly furrowed. During the quiet winter months of 37/38, the 10 acres were levelled and scuffled. Early in 1938 the patch was well manured with well weathered muck, ploughed, and in spring planted with King Edwards. The result in the autumn was a crop that took my father by surprise. The ridged rows were bursting with growing potatoes far larger than normal. The whole country it turned out was awash with potatoes because of the ideal weather conditions.

For many years the Potato Marketing Board had been in existence. Their brief was to regulate an orderly market and this was most easily done by regulating the size of the riddle. This had been introduced in 1935 with some success. The Board therefore in 1938 decreed that potatoes over 1lb in weight should not be sold to retailers and of course, those that fell through the riddle should only be sold as pig potatoes.

I have already briefly described the harvesting of potatoes in the late 1930s with the machine travelling up the rows, throwing out the crop to the waiting women and children who had been allocated perhaps a 10/15 yard patch to clear. They were placed in boxes, collected and laid in a potato clamp, which was a long row, a bit like a boy scouts tent. The row would be covered by straw, then covered by soil dug from the side, which served to keep the straw in place, and provided drainage in wet weather. This ensured they were dry and frost free and the clamp would be opened at one end as the potatoes were needed. They were put through the riddle which sloped slightly so that as the handle was turned, the riddle vibrated. The little potatoes fell through for pig feed, the rest into sacks for sale to retailers. It is only fair to mention that it was not unknown for my Father to have a couple of bricks put under the back legs of the riddle. This altered the rake, the potatoes travelled over the riddle a good deal faster meaning fewer potatoes for pig feed and more in the sacks for sale. So there in a nutshell is the problem. Father maintained, and bear in mind he was prone to exaggerate, that his 1938 crop was one third pig potatoes, one third over a pound in weight and only a third saleable. He therefore ignored the regulations about the big potatoes and continued to sell them.

As the Potato Marketing Board (PMB) inspectors would periodically check up on retail outlets to see if the standard of potatoes on sale – any too small or too big – it was inevitable that, if discrepancies were found, the retailers had to disclose the name of the supplier. This resulted in father being summoned. At first it was a reprimand, but as the transgressions continued, fines were levied. Father complained bitterly to all and sundry and the story began to be reported in the Press.

It became the story of the little farmers against bureaucracy and father's fan mail gathered pace. Fish and chip shops loved big potatoes and the retailers certainly didn't mind passing them on. This battle was regularly reported in the *Lichfield Mercury* and was carried in some National Daily papers – hence the fan mail. Father revelled in the publicity and as things were going well he had the farm lorry emblazoned with a sign showing "Big Potato Towers" with a large potato on either side. The early days of the struggle took place in late 1938 and early 1939 and continued for the following twelve months.

As my father's stubbornness took over, he was continually fined for his transgressions, the fines becoming more severe.

Trading on his success, or notoriety, depending on one's point of view, and following the dressing up of the lorry with the "Big Potato" insignia, Joe Towers now, for the first time in his farming career, had private note paper printed. Inevitably he chose as his telegraphic address "Big Potato Shenstone".

Adding fuel to my father's ego, the film industry also took a fleeting interest. In the 1930s to the 1940s a visit to the cinema in either the afternoon or the evening presented exactly the same programme. The main feature was a film of perhaps an hour and a half and this was supplemented with a second short film of around 30/40 minutes. With forthcoming attractions also advertised, a 10 minute break to purchase ice creams or drinks, the performance lasted around 2½ to 3 hours. An integral part was always a 15 minute review of the national and international news – always interesting as the country approached and subsequently became involved in the War with Germany in September 1939. The two great producers of these news programmes were *Pathe Gazette* and *British Movietone News*. I cannot remember which, but one of them decided to do a short report on the "Big Potato Towers v Potato Marketing Board" conflict. Thus arrangements were made for a camera crew and reporter to visit Home Farm. The potato clamp was opened, the riddle set in place, a worker threw fork loads of potatoes onto the riddle while another turned the handle. Father adopted the pose of the Gentleman farmer surveying the work whilst Pat and I were allowed to hold a watching brief, but well within camera shot. Father was interviewed and as was only to be expected gave a very biased opinion on the merits of his case. Certainly Pat and I spent the next week or so in eager anticipation of seeing our introduction into the film industry and impending stardom. I do not think it vastly changed our lives in the long run, apart from a short term sense of intense disappointment when we eventually went to the cinema to view our starring role only to find we had been edited out. Father meanwhile revelled in the publicity and his ego swelled by the day.

He continued to receive many letters of support over the months and in an attempt to resolve the problem and clear the air a Mr R.W.N. Dawe, a member of the PMB, attended a meeting of the local branch of the National Farmers Union held at the Old Crown Hotel, Lichfield, on the evening of Friday, 20th January 1939. Putting the case for the PMB, he maintained Mr Towers had not been fined for selling big potatoes but for allowing too many small potatoes to be included in a hundred weight bag. Because of the glut, the Board had asked farmers to withhold potatoes over a pound in weight and sell them later in the season. He maintained Mr Towers had adopted a vindictive attitude towards the Board throughout the controversy. He went a stage further by refuting statements made by Mr Towers, which he declared were based on lies.

Mr Dawe pointed out that the National demand for potatoes on average was three and a half to four million tons annually. The National average yield was five to seven million, so some form of control was essential. He also pointed out that a housewife going to buy 1 pound or 2 pounds of potatoes would not be best pleased to be served with one or two potatoes. Mr Dawe went on to say that Mr Towers had not been treated any differently to any other Farmers in the country and there was no reason why he should not abide by the Boards regulations. Although Mr Bower and another local farmer, Mr Foden, had put in a word in defence of my father it had not helped his case by not attending in person. The meeting broke up with Mr Dawe stressing that Mr Towers would have to pay the most recent fine of £10.

When the report of this meeting appeared in the *Lichfield Mercury*, it was inevitable that the paper would seek my father's response. The headline in a subsequent issue read "The answer is a lemon". In an interview he said his crop had been classified by the Boards regulations as one third "pig potatoes", one third over "one pound in weight" leaving him only one third to sell. He stated to the *Mercury* he had no intention of paying the fine and contrary to the Board's assertion, rather than a surplus, he could sell another 50,000 tonnes if he had them.

There is no doubt that my father was receiving many letters of support both from other Farmers and the general public, but, knowing his propensity to exaggerate, his claim that his morning post was similar to the Christmas rush and the Post Office may have to arrange a special service, and the claim that he did not have the time to open all the letters could perhaps be treated with some scepticism. His claim that the farming community was being treated by the Board in much the same way as the Jews were being treated in Germany by Hitler was a little over the top.

As happens with all these struggles which capture the public's attention for a few weeks or even months and which the press thrive on, they eventually fizzle out. The final act was my father suing Mr Dawe for slander following the meeting of the NFU at the Old Crown Hotel, Lichfield on Friday 13th January 1939. Beale & Co, my father's solicitors sent the following statement to the *Lichfield Mercury* with a request from both parties it would be published. It read as follows:

> We are informed that the action which Mr. J.A. Towers of Home Farm, Shenstone, nr Lichfield, commenced against Mr. R.W.N. Dawe of Alrewas Hayes Farm, Fradley, Lichfield, in the High Court claiming damages for slander has been settled. Mr Towers alleged that certain words spoken by Mr Dawe at a meeting of the Lichfield Branch of the NFU held at the Old Crown Hotel, Lichfield on Friday 13th January 1939 were slanderous. At the meeting Mr Dawe explained that the words spoken by him were based on statements attributed to Mr Towers and added that his words would not be justified if Mr Towers did not make the statements attributed to him. Mr Towers denies that he made the statements attributed to him and Mr Dawe accepts Mr Towers denial and agrees that in the circumstances the words spoken by him concerning Mr Towers were not justified.

Chapter 12

War Clouds

With the ending of my father's skirmish with the Potato Marketing Board – it could hardly be called a battle and nothing like the storm clouds building up in Europe – life returned to something near normal at Home Farm. The two farms, Home Farm and Hodge Hill Farm worked well together although Hodge Hill had a finite life. The surrounding area was being developed for housing and the Bradford Estate of which Hodge Hill Farm was part was included in the plans. It was already fragmented with odd fields spreading from the Fox & Goose Public House to Castle Bromwich village. Although horse power of the four-legged variety was still being used, the tractor was coming more and more into its own. The problem of moving the tractor from one farm to the other presented a bit of a problem. Modern tractors hurtle along the road at 30 mph with no difficulty. The old Fordson was more like 10 mph which was an hour's journey from one farm to the other. The solution was to build a ramp at both Farms whereby the lorry could be reversed up to the high point, the tractor driven on to the lorry and transported in a fraction of the time.

On the Home Farm 1939 continued much as before. The usual cereals, potatoes and catch crops of carrots, sprouts, cabbages and the like were grown. Harvesting the wheat and oats was a little easier, although it was still done by the old fashioned binder, but the sheaves were now collected on the lorry. At the age of twelve I had my first lessons in clutch control by driving the lorry along the rows. There was no need to touch the brakes – the lorry stopped as one depressed the clutch and took your foot off the accelerator. This experience stood me in good stead much later in life when I took my driving lessons. A further advantage was the substantial Dutch Barn where the crop could be stored. No need now for the careful building of the ricks out in the open which needed thatching.

There was never any difficulty in selling the produce from the farms, but as the housing estates developed around Hodge Hill Farm, my father had the bright idea of opening a farm shop at Hodge Hill. One of the bays in a building was levelled and the floor concreted. It was a bit Heath Robinson with the shelves made out of packing cases. Bernard was sent off to the Birmingham Market to buy soft fruit to augment the potatoes and vegetables the farm could provide. It was not difficult to undercut the local retailers on the vegetables and the increased margins there meant the soft fruit could also be retailed with a minimum margin. Mother took her turn as part of the staff – I use the term loosely. Bernard and Mary chipped in also as did Pat and I during school holidays. Mother was paid for her efforts – it was one way of getting a bit of cash out of father. All went well and the outlet was profitable until I made a mess of one week's profits. I was on duty with mother who went for a bit of lunch at 12.30 leaving me in charge. The cash box was at the rear of the unit and we also sold bags of lime which was stored 2 or 3 bays away. A family of husband and wife plus 2 children came in, asked if we sold lime. On being assured we did, could they have a 1lb bag. I cannot remember the cost but about 2 or 3 pence in old money. Off I trot with bag and scoop accompanied by husband and two off-springs. Back to the unit, weigh the bag, collect the 2 or 3 pence which I drop into the cash box. Mother returns from lunch 10 minutes later and somewhat anxiously asks what have I done with the £7 which was tucked into the slot at the back of the cash box. Consternation ensues and father suggests mother has pocketed the £7 and made up the story (I wouldn't have blamed her if she had) and she wouldn't be paid until she made it up. I think it all blew over eventually and I was just grateful I got away (not with the £7 let me hasten to add), but without getting my ears boxed. Bernard spent the next 3 lunch breaks concealed in a bay opposite the shop nursing his 12 bore shot gun, in the hope they would return for a second bite, but they were obviously professionals.

As the year progressed, Britain prepared itself for what appeared to be an inevitable conflict with that old adversary Germany. Under Hitler, the country had been building up its armed forces since the early 1930s totally ignoring any restrictions incurred after the 1914/18 conflict. He got away with taking control of the Rhur, Germany's industrial heartland, he annexed Czechoslovakia in 1938 in spite of all Neville Chamberlain's commitment to peaceful negotiations. When German forces marched into Poland in August 1939, Chamberlain had no alternative, after our pledge to Poland, other than to declare "we are now at war with Germany" on September 3rd 1939. Following that momentous declaration nothing much happened. My sister, Pat, had her fourteenth birthday a few days after the outbreak of the war and it was decided that she would finish her scholastic career at that point. A decision with which my sister readily agreed. I'm afraid she was rapidly disillusioned when father told her she would be extremely useful serving in the farm shop at Hodge Hill. As Pat had long ago set her sights on a hairdressing career, this development was not met with a great deal of enthusiasm. This situation continued for the next six months with mother, Pat and me (at the weekends) manning the shop on most days.

By this time a row of 3 or 4 shops had been built in Bucklands End Lane opposite the farm. One was a fruit and vegetable outlet run by the Co-op as I recall and this had a marked effect on our sales. As both farms were profitable, the farm shop was closed down in the early months of 1940 to all our relief, non more that my sister's. With father's approval she now pursued her career in hairdressing by joining the 'Jayne Bennett' salon in the Great Western Arcade in Birmingham as a trainee. One of the regular customers at 'JB' was the Ellison family whom, you will recall, were our landlords at Home Farm. They were resident at Footherley Hall some two or three hundred yards from Home Farm.

Mr Ellison lived there with his wife, his mistress and the three children, an unusual form of cohabitation in those days, and one of which I'm sure my father was most jealous in the light of his affair with Vera. Unfortunately mother did not come from the same mould as Mrs Ellison. The entire female staff of 'JB', particularly the younger inexperienced girls like Pat, were instructed never to be left in a cubicle alone with Mr Ellison. I am told the Ellison family were famous for the parties they used to throw at the Hall with Amy Johnson, the famous flyer, and Elizabeth Welch, a famous black singer, often in residence. Nudity was often on the menu so it seems human nature does not change a great deal over the years. The Hall gardens at the rear were well secluded although they adjoined one of the Home Farm meadows. Pat records it was not unusual in mid-summer to see Mr Ellison wandering around his garden clad in nothing more than a pair of sandals.

In those early months of the war, life went on much as before. I went to King Edwards Grammar School in Lichfield, either by train or bicycle, and as pupils we watched with interest as air raid shelters were built at the edge of the playing fields well away from the school building. We were soon issued with gas masks which became a compulsory part of our school kit.

Chapter 13

The Phoney War

With the declaration of war nothing much happened on land or in the air. In France, the Germans were secure behind the Siegfried Line while the Allied Forces were entrenched in the supposedly impregnable Maginot Line. Food rationing was soon introduced and apart from the disappearance of bananas, oranges and the like from the shops, and sweet rationing (perhaps no bad thing as I still have all my own teeth approaching my 85th birthday). We continued to eat well. Poultry was regularly slaughtered for the weekend meal. Eggs were plentiful and a pig was sent to the Abattoir and mother turned some of the carcass into bacon, although I always found it a bit too salty for my taste. We still produced some milk from a much reduced herd and a limited amount of butter was made to supplement the rationing.

At school (King Edwards, Lichfield) an appeal was made to provide funds to help build a Spitfire. A raffle was organised and as children we were encouraged to take books of tickets home to sell to family and friends. I suspect tickets were three pence or sixpence each and my father now revealed the more magnanimous side of his Jekyll & Hyde character. His favourite watering hole was the 'Blue Ball' on the A5127 (Lichfield to Sutton road). Still revelling in his 'Big Potato' image, he sold my allocation in one night, gave me the money and the counterfoils to take back to school with instructions to bring back more tickets. Over the next week or so he sold more tickets at the 'Blue Ball' and at the 'Bull' in Shenstone village than the rest of my class combined. I became extremely popular with my form Master (whose name escapes me) but perhaps not so much with my class mates as they were harangued as he waved bundles of counterfoils at them saying "look at young Towers, he's setting a fine example!" To further enhance his image, my father also promised a prize of farm produce. True to his word he killed a chicken which mother feathered and dressed. This became the central feature in a suitably lined potato seed tray. This was then surrounded by farm produce including cabbage, cauliflower, carrots, parsnips and of course a bevy of "Big Potatoes". I must confess to a feeling of pride as father drove me to school on the day of the big draw and he carried his gift into the secretary's office. There was a terrible anti-climax when his prize was won by a widow in Lichfield and I was instructed to obtain her name and address so all the buyers of 'my' tickets could be informed.

I rewarded my father in somewhat meagre fashion later. I had been introduced to the Lichfield Boy Scouts by a pal at school. Having joined this meant attending once a week for the usual scouting activities. Rather than cycle back to Footherley some five miles and then back to Lichfield at 6.30 pm or so, I was invited to have tea at my friend's house which saved a 10 mile round trip. It was a bit of a culture shock when after tea, my pal settled down to do 90 minutes of homework! As it was only once a week, I stomached it for the winter months but homework was anathema to me and it would have been a shock to some of the masters at school if young Towers had suddenly soared from his normal 20/22 place out of 24 in the class. Mind you, I could be persuaded to mend my ways. Chemistry was never my favourite subject although I quite enjoyed the experiments. Each week we had to read and learn a chapter from the Chemistry book. A test took place in class and because I had scanned the chapter for 10 minutes before going into the lesson, out of the 20 questions I usually scored in the region of 4 to 8. Enough to keep me out of trouble. Unfortunately on one occasion I failed ignominiously and scored 2 or 3 as I recall. At the end of class I, together with 2 other boys were invited to stay behind and offer some explanation for our abysmal performance. On the spur of the moment I concocted a ridiculous story of my chemistry book falling out of my saddle bag as I cycled home. I suspect the other boys were somewhat more intelligent or honest but we all went over the desk and were suitably chastised across the buttocks with a doubled up piece of rubber tubing. I was last in line and whilst the other two had a 3 a piece, I received 6 of the best. I also suspect he laid into me somewhat more vigorously than the others, probably thinking to himself "I'll teach the little bugger to come up with a better excuse next time". Anyway unlike today with corporal punishment banned, I never breathed a word to my parents. Suffice to say that next week I could virtually recite the first page and a half of the next chapter and recorded my best ever chemistry mark.

So back to my staying in Lichfield for the Scout meeting. As I cycled through the centre of Lichfield, lo and behold, there was father's car in front of me just pulling up.

To my amazement Vera Truelove stepped out of the shadows and off they went.

Because my sister and I had always sided with mother in respect of father's infidelity and not having the perspicacity of my brother who kept his peace when finding father in the chicken house, I could hardly wait to get home and relate to mother what I had seen. No doubt mother and father had words over the situation but on reflection it may have been better to keep silent.

With his publicity re the 'Big Potato' controversy still in the Public's mind, my father took the opportunity to sell seed potatoes to the public. A copy of the advert which appeared in the *Lichfield Mercury* can be seen over the page.

This brought in a welcome cash flow although on a limited time scale.

My father also acquired a small flock of in-lamb ewes in the late Autumn of 1939. It was a one off and I suspect not very remunerative. Welsh farmers seem able to let their sheep roam the hills for much of the year bringing them into cover as lambing time approached. The

ORDER YOUR SEED POTATOES NOW

DON'T DIG FOR VICTORY IN VAIN. **BUY ONLY
SELECTED CERTIFIED ONCE-GROWN SCOTCH SEED.**
THE MINISTRY OF AGRICULTURE INSPECT OUR GROW-
ING POTATOES AND ISSUE CERTIFICATES ONLY TO
SOUND, PURE STOCK.
Do your ground well, plant Certified Seed, and if your potatoes
exceed 1lb. in weight, I guarantee you will get into no trouble
over that.

Varieties on offer—
"KING EDWARD," "GLADSTONE," "GREAT SCOT,"
"DOON EARLY," "BALLYDOON," "DUNBAR ARCHER,"
"KERRS PINK," "DOON STAR," Etc. "Majestic" Sold Out.

CERTIFICATE No. A.T.S.H. (E.) 07116/1940

MINISTRY OF AGRICULTURE &
FISHERIES

**WART DISEASE OF POTATOES
ORDER OF 1923**

The Minister of Agriculture and
Fisheries hereby certifies that the
crop(s) of potatoes of which particu-
lars are given below, grown by Mr. J.
A. Towers, of Home Farm, Shenstone,
Lichfield, Staffs., have been inspected
whilst growing by an Inspector of the
Ministry of Agriculture and Fisheries,
and were then found or believed by the
Inspector to be of the approved immune
varieties undermentioned, true to type
and reasonably free from "rogues,"
and substantially free from severe virus
diseases and wildings.

IN WITNESS whereof the Official
Seal of the Minister of Agriculture and
Fisheries is hereunto affixed this
eleventh day of October, nineteen hundred and forty.

W. DUTTON.

Authorised by the Minister.

J. A. (BIG POTATO) TOWERS
HOME FARM, SHENSTONE
STAFFS.

Advertisement for J.A. Towers, Home Farm.

flock was not really big enough to warrant the acquisition of a specialist sheep dog and anyway neither father nor any of the farm hands were experienced in controlling such a dog.

When they escaped into Footherley Lane, which they seemed to do regularly, it was always an effort to get them back into their designated pasture, so all in all it was a one season wonder. Anyway bigger problems were looming on the horizon but more of that later. Perhaps Pat and I enjoyed the lambing process more than most. Almost inevitably there would be a lamb or two born when the mother for some reason had difficulty in feeding their offspring. This resulted in hand-feeding from a bottle and I doubt if there is a more fascinating and rewarding pastime than that. The lambs rapidly became pets and it was a sorry day when they had grown enough to become self-sufficient.

Chapter 14

Warning Signs

As 1939 ended and we moved into 1940 very little changed in respect of the local farming community.

This was not so in the wide world community. Chamberlain's days as Prime Minister were numbered and Winston Churchill was brought back into the Cabinet as First Lord of the Admiralty. Butter, bacon, sugar and meat were rationed. Petrol prices rose and that too became rationed.

Meanwhile in France, the German army safely ensconced behind the Siegfried line faced the French and British Forces equally secure behind the supposedly impregnable Maginot Line.

With typical German ruthlessness, they solved this apparent insoluble problem by invading Holland and Belgium, sweeping round the rear of the Allied defences and leading to our evacuation of Europe.

While operation "Dynamo", as Dunkirk was named at the time was a disaster, it also represented a remarkable victory in a way, as 340,000 troops were rescued from the beaches by an armada of small boats supported by the navy between 27th May and 4th June.

Later in the year, the Battle of Britain commenced when the German Air Force attempted to obtain control of British air space by eliminating our Air Force. The result has been recorded in many publications and has gone down in history forever to be remembered in Churchill's speech "Never has so much been owed".

Failure to eliminate Fighter Command led Goering, Chief of the German Air Force, to change tack and switch his attack to London and subsequently to the industrial heartland in the Midlands and various major ports. These attacks continued until 1941 when Hitler turned his attention to Russia and in retrospect bit off more than he could swallow.

I only mention the conflict with Germany because it opened up a couple of profitable side-lines for my father.

First we had a substantial five-bedroomed house with three reception rooms in a comparatively secure environment. We didn't exactly become a B/B establishment but with the Castle Bromwich area home to the Aerodrome and the spitfire factory across the road, Dunlop's next door and GEC, English Electric and ICI not far away, the area presented an attractive target to the Luftwaffe.

It was not surprising that some people were keen to escape the area at night (most bombing raids were night time attacks) so father was happy to make a room available for a modest charge on the understanding they arrived late and left early, with toilet facilities the only extra.

However the temporary letting of the spare rooms was a mere sprat in comparison to the mackerel he landed within the next few weeks.

As I have previously mentioned, my father was not one for staying in at nights. At Hodge Hill Farm, the limited accommodation provided enough incentive not to stay in, particularly with two young children making a nuisance of themselves. At Footherley, the incentive was Vera plus his local fame as "Big Potato Towers". Combine these with his ability to tell a good story and the declining relationship with mother and it was no surprise he could be found more often than not in the Blue Ball at Wood End on the A38 or the Bull at Shenstone.

It was in the Blue Ball that a chance encounter with some senior management of a couple of manufacturing firms in the Castle Bromwich/Aston area or 'Bomb Alley' as it could be called, led to his next stroke of good fortune.

It transpired that a "safe haven" in the countryside was needed to store replacement machine tools, generators and such like, in case bomb damage caused disruption in production – something the country could ill afford.

Father had spare buildings and the Luftwaffe were hardly likely to target Shenstone, let alone Footherley. The next week or so saw buildings being spruced up. The cow sheds or milking parlour, to give it its proper title, were hosed down and every day I came home from school, it appeared a new piece of machinery had taken up residence. They were all securely wrapped, the companies were happy enough to pay for the privilege of knowing any interruption to production could probably be solved with no great difficulty.

Joe Towers was therefore batting on a very good wicket. It was suggested, the income from the engineering letting side was not far short of covering the rent on the farm. One would think that in that sort of situation, and in view of the fact that his tenancy was for a period of 5 years, you would go out of your way to stay on the right side of your landlord. Father's stubborn belief in his own security and perhaps a degree of egotism ensured he would go on figuratively speaking "ploughing his own furrow". He was soon to learn the error of his ways.

Chapter 15

Notice to Quit

In the early months of 1939, Mr Ellison had asked father's permission to show a Mr Burton over the farm and a cursory look over the farmhouse itself. Difficult to say no to the request to view the acreage and perhaps in an attempt to placate our landlord, Mr Burton was shown over Home Farm. The result was not particularly beneficial to my father as Mr Burton fell in love with the place. He let it be known to Mr Ellison, he would be more than happy to take over the lease if Mr Ellison would consider giving my father notice to quit.

In the summer of 1940 Ellison did just that: all very legal and in accordance with the terms of the lease. As I have already put on record, relations between my father and Mr Ellison had never been very cordial and as a landlord acting well within his rights, he had no intention of relenting.

Whether my father could have accepted the situation and searched for another farm is open to conjecture. He certainly did not wish to move too far away as it could lead to complications with his affair with Vera for a start and, anyway, his financial position was reasonably sound with the sub-letting of the premises. It should be recorded that mother was no great beneficiary of this largesse and getting money out of father was a bit like trying to get blood out of a stone. It was often my sister's task to try and prise open the coffers if mother wanted a pre-Christmas shopping expedition, but even Pat's appeal fell on stony ground more often than not.

My father regularly consulted Beale & Co, his Birmingham based solicitors, but unfortunately their advice did not concur with what he wanted to hear. Mr Ellison was acting well within his rights and you should make plans to vacate Home Farm by the middle of 1941 was their verdict.

Rubbish was my father's response. I'm a bloody good farmer. I'm making a solid contribution to the nation's need for food, failing to mention he was having it off with a local lass and any move would complicate his extramarital affair.

Perhaps in a fit of pique, he then embarked on a policy designed, if it was not already in the stars, to alienate Mr Ellison even more.

You will recall that Home Farm's 120 acres was split around half and half either side of Footherley Lane. The northern side contained the house, all the farm buildings and arable land apart from a meadow and orchard looking to the west. On the other side of the road it was all meadowland down to the brook and meadows the other side, with perhaps 20 acres of arable land beyond that.

With Footherley Hall also on the south side of Footherley Lane, the gardens looked over the grassland and the brook, producing a pleasant pastoral scene. One which Mr Ellison was eager to preserve. Whilst my father left the 10 acres of grassland adjoining Footherley Hall, he proceeded to plough 20 acres to the east including a rabbit warren that had existed for years. He had no need of the meadow land with the disappearance of the dairy herd and it would be more use to the nation growing a cereal, not to mention far more profitable from his point of view.

There was the inevitable dispute with Mr Ellison. Even Government Ministers got involved with my father claiming that Lord Woolton, the then Minister for Food and Mr Hudson, Minister for Agriculture, both giving their approval. Others thought he had ploughed without the proper approval, but it seemed to make no difference. Even to this day, 75 years later, that 20 acres is still under the plough, but more often now the yellow blossom of oil seed rape can be seen. Father obtained a lot more publicity which gave him a few more stories to regale his friends with at the 'Blue Ball' and the 'Bull'.

Chapter 16

Annus Horribilis

Part I

It is probably no great exaggeration to say that, while the Queen suffered her ghastly year in 1992 when Royal Marriages broke down and a Royal Castle suffered drastic damage, the year 1941 became the Towers nightmare.

The year started well enough with father launching an advertising campaign in the *Lichfield Mercury* to sell his "King Edward seed potatoes" trading on his battle with the Potato Marketing Board of a couple of years previously. He had also taken the opportunity to launch an appeal, at the end of the previous year, to local residents in Lichfield and surrounding areas to raise £100 to send to Russia for arms in support of their desperate struggle against the Germans. The article which appeared in the *Mercury* was as follows:

> There was also a report from the Lichfield Gardens and Allotments Society that "following their show they had made a profit of £20, which the Society had divided between the local Red Cross and the Mayors Relief Fund. J. A. (Big Potato) Towers of Home Farm Shenstone gave Five Tons of Potatoes to readers of the Mercury to promote his selected certified once grown Scotch seed sug-

gesting, if the reader dug his ground well and planted certified seed, he might get potatoes exceeding 1lb. in weight and he guaranteed that the gardener would get into no trouble over that from the Minister of Agriculture."

He still couldn't resist having a dig at the Authorities even a couple of years later!

While I continued my schooling at King Edwards in Lichfield, my sister Pat, was revelling in learning the hair dressing trade at Jayne Bennetts. She recalls the first year in 1940 as one where she learned the art of shampooing and drying. One might have thought she would have been alienated as many of her duties included mopping the entrance to the salon every morning and making tea or coffee for the less well-off clients. But for those of substantial wealth, it meant going 50 yards up New Street to Pattisons and bringing back the Pot of Tea or Coffee on a silver tray, top quality china cups and a selection of biscuits. The whole salon had to be evacuated periodically as the Air Raid warning sounded over Birmingham. The nearest refuge was next door where there was a Snooker Club in the basement which provided reasonably secure short term protection.

Pat will forgive me when I say that, as a school girl, she was not the best looker in the class. However as she blossomed at 'JB' and became accustomed to mixing with the "upper crust" as it were, she became a very attractive auburn-haired lass. It became natural that at the weekends, a trip to Sutton to the cinema became a weekly occasion. Originally, to placate father, these trips were to meet girlfriends but it was not long before young lads were taking an interest. One young man by the name of John Cartwright was smitten and one weekend, when at the same cinema he had seen Pat with a girlfriend, he patiently waited for my sister to come out. That started a friendship which ran for some years. His visits to Home Farm created very much the right impression, particularly on mother and subsequently on father as well. John volunteered for the RAF and qualified as a pilot officer in 1942. Regrettably he was reported missing on an operation over the sea in

Pat Towers, aged 18.

1943 and his body was never recovered. I always recall on one visit to the Farm, I showed him an incendiary bomb which I had picked up in one of our fields. It had obviously been dropped from a German plane and, landing in soft ground, had failed to ignite – not that it would have done any damage anyway. The device had sat on the mantelpiece in my bedroom for some months with no repercussions. On this particular visit John ventured the opinion that it was not really appropriate and on that basis he took the bomb outside and to my amazement, unscrewed the bottom and sprinkled the contents on the brick courtyard where Pat and I had learned to hit a tennis ball against the garage door. When he had spread the powder in a circle he then struck a match and set the circle on fire. The result was quite remarkable and, if not like bonfire night, at least it brought it home to me, how dangerous something like that could be when dropped in a built up area. I could well understand the necessity for fire fighters to be encouraged to volunteer in towns and cities and particularly in industrial areas.

In spite of being under notice to quit, life went on at Home Farm much as usual. The land was prepared for Spring planting and the usual 30 acres or so of seed.

Potatoes were planted as were some 20/30 acres of grain and a lesser amount of land devoted to catch crops, carrots, cabbage, sprouts and peas, etc.

All this normal farming activity was taking place under the cloud of the "notice to quit" which was due to expire in early June, only three months away. While superficially my father appeared to be living in "cloud cuckoo land", he continued to ignore all the advice of Beale & Co, his solicitors, and remained firmly convinced it would eventually be proved he had security of tenure and all would be well.

While, as I have said, planting went on, he was continuing to sow his own seed fairly regularly as he had been doing for many years. Whether by luck or other means (the contraceptive pill was still a distant dream in the mind of the more liberated members of both sexes), my father had succeeded in avoiding the complications of an unwanted pregnancy. His luck ran out in March when Vera became pregnant, although it was July before it was impossible to hide the obvious. The news was greeted in the Truelove household as an absolute disaster. They may have been at the lower levels in the social scale of things, having worked in the kitchens at Footherley Hall and toiled in the fields as farm labourers, but they had fairly strict views from a moral point of view and not getting pregnant outside of marriage was one of them.

Vera was evicted in summary fashion and inevitably she turned to father. He in turn approached old friends in Castle Bromwich who agreed to look after Vera until the baby was born. The next six months were an absolute nightmare for the poor girl. Cut off from her family, no friends in Castle Bromwich and father some ten miles away – not two hundred yards as it had been for the past four years – she endured a miserable time. The baby was eventually born on the 2nd January 1942, but much water was to flow under the bridge before the turn of the year.

Chapter 17

Annus Horribilis

Part II

Before Vera was thrown out, father had to face the termination of his 12 months notice to get out of Home Farm. Inevitably all sorts of legal activity was taking place. The possibility of reconciliation between Mr Ellison and my father was non-existent and ultimately, as a last resort, the notice to quit was extended for a further six months.

Perhaps this extension furthered my father's belief that the problem had been solved and so we continued to run the farm as though all was well in the world. He visited Vera as and when he could, but faced with a 20 mile round trip and petrol rationing, it is no exaggeration to say it was not as often as Vera would have wished. With the six month extension to the lease at Home Farm, the late summer of 1941 continued in much the same vein as usual. The corn was harvested but the tradition of building ricks out in the open had been forsaken and the Dutch Barn was used eliminating the necessity for "thatching". Potatoes were "got" as in those days "potato getting" was the usual term for lifting the crop. As usual I was employed as cheap labour in the school holidays, and if an extra pair of hands were needed, I was called upon even in school term. A short note to the school recording an indisposition of some sort was all that was needed.

Pat, as a working girl, was exempt from farm labouring. Even my father could no longer send a note to her employer as my sister drew the line at being a "land army girl". She had served her apprenticeship at Jayne Bennetts and had by this time qualified as a fully-fledged stylist. She had earlier applied for, and obtained, a position at Harry Bryans salon at the "Tudor Rose" in Sutton Coldfield.

Although my father still had this firm belief that he had security of tenure, perhaps there was an element of doubt creeping in. This was reflected in the fact that the upkeep of the farm was not on the same scale as previously. The most noticeable aspect was the fact that the grass tennis court was suddenly put out of action with the introduction of half a dozen sows on to it. Whilst it had never been kept up to Wimbledon or even local club standards, it had been good enough to provide many hours of enjoyment with family and friends. All done without the aid of motorised mowers!

The front garden and the 9 hole putting green which wended its way between the various flower beds, whilst neglected in 1941, was not "put to the sword" by the introduction of the pigs, although I suspect my father was sorely tempted.

So, as autumn faded and winter fast approached, Pat and I continued our lives in complete and utter ignorance of looming disaster. I doubt if even Bernard at Hodge Hill Farm was fully aware and I suppose mother was kept informed, but had no say in the matter anyway.

While not exactly "Armageddon", father's battle with Mr Ellison came to a head on Tuesday 16th December 1941. I can do no better than record the event as reported in the *Lichfield Mercury* as follows:

TURNED OFF HIS FARM ON HIGH SHERIFF'S WRIT
NOW HOMELESS AND OUT OF WORK

Passers-by in a quiet country lane near Shenstone on Tuesday must have experienced a sense of unusual curiosity by the spectacle of a group of press photographers, journalists and policemen gathering in the proximity of Home Farm, Footherley. This, as probably the majority of our readers are aware is, or rather was, the domicile of Mr J. A. (Big Potato) Towers and the cause of the excitement we are now able to reveal, was the execution of a High Court Order for ejectment by the Sheriff's Officer for the County. The latter was accompanied by two assistants. The officer (Mr Charles Davenhill) duly armed with his warrant, which had been granted in the Walsall County Court in favour of Footherley Estates Ltd, the owners of the house and farm.

A Unique Story

When a *Mercury* representative arrived on the scene, he was courteously received by Mr Towers and ushered into his dining room. There assembled, he found a number of London and fellow Birmingham journalists and photographers, including a cinematograph representative, all of whom had anticipated a unique story.

It had been assumed that the Sheriff and his men would place the whole of the stock on the farm onto the main road as part of the executive order. Whether the sight of dozens of pigs and hundreds of fowl running about loose on the farm premises created too formidable an operation we are not aware, but suffice to say the Sheriffs officer announced that this part of the day's proceedings would be dispensed with. Another formality he dispensed with was the removal of the furniture, but this apparently did not meet with the approval of the representative of the solicitor for the plaintiffs.

At last the Sheriff's Officer announced that he desired everyone off the premises and Mr Towers and his family, together with the newsmen and cameramen made their way into the farmyard. Outside tractors were ordered to a standstill whilst ploughing was in progress. The employees were asked to leave the farm which they did in company with the horses. Mr Towers told the *Mercury* representative that he had nowhere to move his farm stock and belongings to. "I am making a stand on behalf of all farmers in the country who are tenants" he said. "If after improving a farm, a man can be given notice to get out whether he likes it or not, I think it is an injustice to farmers who are making an all important contribution to the war effort today."

Increased Yield From £800 To £5,000

"I took over this farm five years ago when it was in a dilapidated condition and have made such a good job of it that the owners congratulated me several times. I had been promised a five year lease and then a yearly tenancy, but last year I received twelve months' notice to get out. That was, I contend, for no reason whatever, as I have always paid my rent and do not owe a farthing."

Mr Towers went on to say that during the time he had been at the farm he had increased the yield on foodstuffs from a value of £800 to £5,000 per year. There was today £6,000 worth of stock on the premises. He had orders for 200 tons of potatoes at £10 a ton for certified seed, had four clover ricks, £2,500 worth of potatoes on the farm, 500 head of poultry, 50 pigs, five work horses, four cattle, £1,000 worth of tractors, lorries and implements to work a 150 acre farm. There was still five days threshing to be done and new crops had already been sown. Continuing his conversation, Mr Towers said "Today I leave the lot where it is because I have nowhere to move it and I am out of work for the first day in my life. I have been unable to get another farm. The sun was at last beginning to shine for agriculture and I was looking forward to better times."

"The farm consists of 146 acres but 26 are woodland. The rent of the 120 acres of workable land Mr Towers said was therefore approximately £2 per acre which was probably as much as that charged to any farmer in Staffordshire."

Several employees have been thrown out of work but we understand that Mr Towers has promised them their wages until such time as he could fix something up for them. Among them was 73 year old George Hitchcox who worked for Mr Tower's father and grandfather.

No Explanation For Eviction

Mr Towers and his family are staying at the George Hotel for a few days and yesterday told our representative that during the whole of the time negotiations were in progress he was never seen with regard to staying on at the farm and when he went to see his landlord to approach him on the matter, he said he would not see him. Mr Towers said he then wrote a very pleading letter but that had not been answered to this day. Nothing was said to him about leaving until all the potatoes were camped and all the ricks securely thatched. Then they came and asked him when he was going to get out.

Asked about the feeding of the livestock, Mr Towers said as far as he knew the plaintiffs in the action, the Footherley Estates Ltd, were responsible for the feeding and maintenance of the stock. If he went back himself he had been told it would be contempt of court.

Knowing my father's penchant for exaggeration, some of the figures quoted above can be taken with the proverbial pinch of salt. Suffice to say, sometime after lunch, father, mother, Pat and I were escorted off the premises. True to his word we booked in at the George Hotel which was a bit of a novelty as any holidays had always been with mother alone and invariably this involved a boarding house of somewhat limited pretentions. Father's statement that we would be staying there for the time being turned out to be one night! Mother, Pat and I headed for her side of the family. Father, I assume, to his.

Chapter 18

Nomads

With the eviction from Home Farm, father had insisted that we depart with the things we stood up in. Mother was instructed to leave all our personal possessions behind but fortunately she had the good sense to at least pack all the necessities for an overnight stay in the hotel. We departed to the George Hotel in Lichfield in what can only be described as a muted blaze of publicity, where we stayed for approximately 24 hours.

The following morning father paid the bill and it was agreed we three, mother, Pat and I would seek temporary refuge with mother's relations while father would make his own arrangements. He was still suffering under the grand illusion that someone sitting in an office in London would wave a magic wand, rule that a great injustice had been committed, and accompanied by a fanfare of trumpets we would be reinstated into Home Farm in triumph. In reality pigs would be flying across the sky in droves before that was ever going to happen. So father made off on his own while we three made our way to Lichfield railway station heading for Lytham House High School and the ever welcoming bosom of Auntie Louie, mother's eldest sister. School holidays for Christmas were about to start so the situation at Lytham House would be fairly relaxed and mother had already ascertained that we would be welcome albeit on a temporary basis. On arriving at Erdington railway station, it was only a short walk to the school in Shortheath Road where, as always, we were made welcome. Mother's first task was to establish contact with Mr Ellison on our behalf to seek permission to have access to Home Farm just to collect the personal items of clothing, etc. This was granted under supervision, so mother and I plus a borrowed van plus driver collected all our clothes and three bicycles. Pat meanwhile returned to work at "Tudor Rose", having had a few days off, where Harry Bryan had been very co-operative during these unusual circumstances.

So, whilst we bedded down to "enjoy" a different sort of Christmas, father went from pillar to post cadging accommodation as and where he could. Perhaps the one bright spot to come out of all this was the fact that he could at least spend a bit more time with Vera who was now in the final stages of her pregnancy. Whilst the family Vera was staying with in Castle Bromwich had been most charitable, they drew the line at having my father staying the night. Not that he spent all day and every day with Vera. Her pregnancy had always been looked upon as a bit of an encumbrance for which he held the poor girl entirely responsible.

Christmas approached and it soon became patently obvious that restoration back into Home Farm was never going to happen. By this time the house had been stripped of the entire contents which were stored in various outbuildings.

The Christmas of 1941, in the annals of history, will not be regarded as one of the greatest for the Towers family. In the past traditional get-togethers in front of coal fires with present opening for all had been the norm. We celebrated Christmas Day with Auntie Louie and her family but with no great present opening ceremony. What money mother had saved over the years would be needed to finance our search for fresh accommodation in the New Year. I suspect mother was resigned to the fact that this latest trauma signalled the end of the marriage which had not been the happiest for some years.

However, if our Christmas had been a bit different than usual, one could almost feel a bit of sympathy for my father, in spite of the fact that it was his stubbornness that had landed the family in its current situation. On leaving the George Hotel, there was never any question of him being made welcome at Lytham House. As I have already mentioned, there was never a great rapport between the Towers and the Pywell families.

Over Christmas and the New Year he survived, but that period proved to be almost too much for Vera. Her delivery date was fast approaching and the pregnancy had not been an easy one. In the late months of 1941, on the run up to Christmas, she had been in and out of hospital. The people she had been living with had been remarkably good with her but they had their own lives to lead and consequently Vera spent many hours alone.

Eventually she went into labour on the first of January giving birth to a son on the second of January 1942 at Hill House Lane in the district of Yardley. On receipt of the news, my father called to see Vera and in no uncertain terms told her the baby must be adopted. Vera had no choice in the matter. She had always been dominated by my father so the orphanage was approached, the matter approved, and within hours the baby was taken away by my father and delivered to the appropriate institution.

That as far as he was concerned was the end of the matter. The mere fact that for the next few weeks Vera was close to suicide was a matter of indifference to him. As it turned out he had more important matters to concern him looming on the horizon. Not everyone agreed with that opinion.

Chapter 19

Incarceration

With the baby problem solved my father turned his attention to finding lodgings for Vera. At this stage it seemed he still had hopes that he would be reinstated at Home Farm. He therefore felt his chances would be improved if he stayed in the vicinity of Footherley. From various records it can be confirmed that he took up residence at "The Bungalow" in Shenstone. I can be fairly certain this would be as a lodger, but whether with a family or one of his former lady friends is a matter of conjecture. He certainly was not short of money for he was still running his Rover car which he desperately needed, not only to keep in touch with Vera but to retain his mobility in a rural area.

It is difficult to pin point accurately what he was up to in the Spring and Summer of 1942 but he surfaced in the Autumn. At that time the Government encouraged every district to become self-contained units with the object of maintaining morale and to provide funds for the RAF.

Joe Towers approached the Editor of the *Lichfield Mercury* with the proposal that a Darts Competition be held during the winter months. Darts was a pastime in most public houses and it was felt that many players would enjoy the possibility of pitting their skills against different people. He would provide £25 in prize money – £20 for the winner and £5 for the runner up. An entrance fee of 1 shilling (20 shillings to the pound for those readers who have only lived in this decimal age.) This would be one of the biggest cash prizes ever to have been presented in this sport or so my father maintained. It would be a knock out competition and any player who had won a former competition outside his own Pub would be barred. Licensees or the steward would collect the entry forms which should be returned to the Fox and Hounds in Shenstone. A closing date was decided and the draw made on a local basis to restrict travelling too far and the licensee/steward submitting the most entrants would receive a Christmas Hamper provided by Mr Towers. As my father said, "the proceeds will go to the RAF to provide bombs to blast those Nazis nitwits out of their nests". During September/October the number of entrants rose rapidly and finally totalled around 5,000 with most of the pubs in the Staffordshire and West Warwickshire area being represented. The competition proceeded well with the local winners being announced around Christmas. The winner of the Christmas hamper was a Mrs B Clark of the Horse & Jockey in Sandford St, Lichfield and Joe Towers had much pleasure in making the presentation. The semi-finals were completed in February 1943 with the final taking place in the Guild Hall on the 29th March between Mr. C Shorthouse (New Inns) and Mr L Bowden (Royal Oak) with Mr Bowden coming out on top. My father was given the job of announcer for the evening and received a round of applause whilst the Mayor gave everyone a vocal pat on the back.

By this time, I am sure my father had resigned himself that any possibility of a return to Home Farm was out of the question. Indeed the farm had a new occupant in a Mr Burton who had taken over the tenancy earlier in the year.

Meanwhile my father had not let his darts competition distract him from paying attention to Vera. He saw her regularly, taking her out to the pictures and she in turn satisfied his sexual needs. Inevitably Vera ended up pregnant again, but more of that later.

Still residing at the Bungalow my father became involved with some litigation with Footherley Estates. I can only presume that this involved non-payment of the farm rent which he probably withheld as eviction approached. Any decision was withheld in Birmingham as the farm and

Footherley Hall were both in Staffordshire and it was subsequently heard in Lichfield. The result, whatever it was, went against my father – this was in June 1943 – and somewhere around this time, either Footherley Estates or my father started bankruptcy proceeding. Dates here become fuzzy. There appears to be 100 year embargo on researching such history!

Most readers will know, but not I trust through bitter experience that when you plead poverty, the courts will want proof that this is the case. As the legal steamroller continued its pedestrian progress, I have no doubt my father felt so aggrieved over his treatment by officials of the law that when asked to provide details of all his assets, he was not entirely accurate in his disclosures.

Whether he forgot to say he still had a car or more likely did not disclose a bank or building society account, I do not know, but what is certain is the fact he was found out and was summoned to appear at Birmingham Crown Court on a charge of dishonesty and failure to disclose in full his assets.

I do not think a great sum was involved. Perhaps there had been friction between the Plaintiff and my father in the past and this was his chance to get back at that "big headed sod from Home Farm". Anyway in this day and age some seventy years later, I am sure there would have been a fine, a slap on the wrist and away you go. As it was my father received a severe dressing down and, like Norman Fletcher (alias Ronnie Barker) in Porridge, he heard the dreaded pronouncement "You will go to prison for nine months".

Perhaps in the dim and distant past there have been other members of the Towers clan who have been guests of His or Her Majesty's institutions, but I have not been able to trace any. The shock waves throughout both families were substantial and I suspect the Wells family, being such pillars of society, were not best pleased. These days a year or two in prison seems to present the miscreant with the opportunity to write a best seller while incarcerated, or perhaps an autobiography on one's release, but anyway it does not seem to carry the same stigma these days.

Chapter 20

Temporary Accommodation

Whilst my father had been fighting his losing battle with the authorities, my mother had naturally enough, reached the obvious conclusion that we could not stay at Lytham House indefinitely. Early in the new year we began a search for new accommodation. The fact that the new school term started in early January 1942 made it even more imperative we made a move. Auntie Louie had been more than generous over the Christmas period and now it became the turn of one of mother's other sisters Cecelia Skolastica (forever known as Auntie Cissy) to offer us temporary refuge. Auntie Cissy lived in a modest three-bedroomed property in Sheffield Road, Erdington and was married to Uncle Bert. They were childless and had a couple of spare bedrooms and as they both worked the house was empty for most of the day.

The property was in fact owned by Grandfather Pywell. Like the Towers family he had been a tenant farmer all his life but unlike my father, he had always taken good care of his money, ending up with a substantial number of modest properties.

Mother's search for rented accommodation proved fruitful in late January when she was put in touch with Mrs Hughes who lived at 186 Birmingham Road, Wylde Green, Sutton Coldfield. She lived in a substantial Victorian property, so we had the use of the lounge at the front of the house plus the front bedroom which mother and Pat shared whilst I had the middle bedroom. Mrs Hughes used the rest of the house while mother obviously had access to the kitchen facilities.

What little money mother had saved over the years was not going to last forever, so employment for me and also mother herself became a priority. It was not difficult in those days to find a job and as many of the Pywell clan had always taken a cautious approach to investment, their favourite haven had for many years been the "Birmingham Incorporated Building Society". Mother got in touch with them to see if they had a vacancy for a "promising" (some poetic licence here) fifteen year old lad and after an interview where, it seemed, I did nothing wrong, I started my business career at the end of January, with a starting salary of £2-10 a week. It didn't take mother long to obtain a position with the General Post Office where she ended up in the section sorting out incoming mail from America for the USA troops stationed in England. Pat meanwhile was now earning reasonable money at Tudor Rose and, while I would never admit it to her face was developing into a very attractive auburn haired girl. She was also gathering a rich and well-connected clientele based in Four Oaks, Streetly and Little Aston, these being the more affluent areas of Sutton Coldfield. The connection proved to be extremely important in mid-June. Pat had a hair appointment with a Mrs Jones who lived in Hartopp Road on the Four Oaks Estate. During her shampoo and set, in conversation with Pat, Mrs Jones mentioned that she had seen in the paper that the contents of Home Farm, Footherley, late residence of 'Big Potato' Towers were being put up for auction on the Friday of that week. This news came to Pat on the Tuesday. On the Wednesday evening, having been put in the picture by Pat, mother went to see her father and borrowed £50, and thus armed, arranged with the GPO to have Friday off.

The auction took place at 12 noon, the contents of the house having been placed in the field opposite to the entrance. Mother arrived early and managed to get an appointment with Mr Winterton, the Auctioneer. She pleaded that some of the contents were in fact her property and with the cooperation of the auctioneers was able to select a number of items which were put on one side. In addition he made a note of various pieces which mother was interested in and when these came under the hammer, they were knocked down to mother's bid perhaps a little more quickly than should have been the case.

Wintertons also offered a storage facility, and mother arranged for her purchases to go into store in Lichfield, pending permanent accommodation being found. Following this expedition, we now had the fundamentals to set up home in due course. If Pat never made another contribution to our well-being in the future, she had certainly earned her corn with this piece of information.

Chapter 21

Another Reconciliation

During the summer of 1943 we continued our tenancy at 186 Birmingham Road. It was convenient for Pat and mother, who both worked in Sutton Coldfield, whilst the bus to Birmingham stopped opposite 186.

Pat and I were never encouraged to visit father in Winson Green – perhaps he had no wish to be humiliated – but mother must have been in touch. It would have been easy enough whilst Pat and I were at work. At least, that must be the assumption because on his release he came knocking on the door of 186. But more of that later.

The summer meandered on whilst I enjoyed learning a bit about the business world of investment and borrowing. Only one fly in the ointment. The triumvirate of Messrs. Pearson, Trevelyn and Jones who ran the Birmingham Incorporated Building Society (BIBS) were adamant that, if I was going to make my mark in this sphere, passing the appropriate exams in Book Keeping, Economics and Building Society Laws and Practice was mandatory. As I have mentioned earlier, I saw my future in farming and felt no urge to study too hard. I was playing football and table tennis for the Abbey RC Church Youth Club. This was far more important than swotting, and anyway the BIBS wanted me to purchase all the necessary books out of my own pocket and study in my own time. On the credit side the hours were not too onerous. Opening at 9 a.m., the doors closed at 3 p.m. and, as long as the cashiers balanced, one could be away by 4 p.m. It was always interesting to go into Birmingham and see what part of the City Centre had been decimated by the German bombers. They made a mess of New St., opposite the Odeon Cinema, I recall, but Waterloo St. survived pretty well.

Once the cashiers had balanced, the cash elements were put into small leather bags which locked, and the Chief Cashier would take them across to the Midland Bank in Temple Row and deposit them in the night safe. I was often delegated to accompany him as a security guard! I'm not quite sure what use I would have been as I was a fairly slender youth and had no pretentions to be a 'have a go hero' had we been attacked. Fortunately we were never put to the test.

So the summer passed and in September my father was released having had three months knocked off his sentence for good behaviour. He had survived his six months in Winson Green with equanimity, and concealing one's assets in a Bankruptcy was considered fair game amongst the other residents. In addition he was a good raconteur and was able to entertain his fellow detainees with some of the stories related in this publication. I suspect they were much embellished and perhaps that is where one of his granddaughters gets it from. It was something of a surprise when I arrived home one afternoon to find him sitting in the lounge. This was never going to be a happy reunion and I have always wondered why mother bothered to tell him where we were living.

Perhaps the story of the missing £100 had something to do with it. As youngsters Pat and I were inevitably dragged into it. It appeared that before his court case, one of his friends had given father a car to sell. He wanted a certain sum for it, perhaps £100 or so, and anything he got for it, over and above that figure, father could keep for himself. The result was a surplus of £100 which he kept as agreed, and he maintained he gave it to mother to keep on his behalf. Mother denied all knowledge of this and one can imagine the atmosphere was a bit fraught. With nowhere to go for the night, father was allowed to sleep in the lounge, but without the knowledge or permission of Mrs Hughes. It was not easy to conceal his presence, and the balloon went up the following morning when they met in the hall and she threatened to set the dog onto him. Rags (the dog) could be an unfriendly brute at the best of times, and I always had to mind my P's and Q's when he was around. Fortunately it didn't come to that, but father departed minus the mysterious £100, and as you can imagine, somewhat disgruntled.

My sympathies over the years had always been with my mother, but I suspect she was not being entirely honest on this occasion. She may well have pocketed the lot and considered it as compensation for my father's infidelity, and I would not have blamed her. More likely perhaps, she would have repaid some of his debts or perhaps have donated it to the Church.

Anyway that finally put an end to the marriage. It also soured relations with Mrs Hughes and prompted mother to seek other accommodation. Before we departed 186, one aspect always stays in my mind. I have already mentioned Pat had grown into a good looking girl. Inevitably, the local lads buzzed around and didn't seem put off by our temporary accommodation. On this particular Saturday afternoon Pat had three suitors all call within fifteen minutes of each other. I took enormous glee out of ushering each one into the lounge, which was becoming quite crowded by the time number three arrived, and seeing Pat attempting to wriggle out of a somewhat embarrassing situation.

I understand my father made his way to Hodge Hill Farm seeking shelter, and readers will make their own minds up as to where their sympathies lie when I say he was given short shrift by his daughter-in-law. Mary told him in no uncertain terms he was not welcome in the farmhouse but could sleep in the barn if he so wished. I understand he stayed a couple of nights before he eventually found the consoling arms of Vera. But that is for later.

Chapter 22

Intermezzo

At this stage, with father written out of the equation as it were, it seems sensible to donate a few pages to the rest of the Towers family i.e. mother, Bernard, Pat and myself. With relations with Mrs Hughes at a low point it was mutually agreed we would find alternative accommodation as soon as possible.

We already had the furniture, rescued from the sale at Home Farm, at 186 Lichfield Road, so the ideal solution would be to find a small three-bedroomed house of our own.

An approach to Grandfather Pywell brought forth the promise of a deposit if we could find the right place. This subsequently produced, after much searching, 108 Mere Green Road, a modest semi-detached residence. Mere Green is a suburb of Sutton Coldfield, on the Lichfield side, and perhaps is best described as the poor relation of Four Oaks. However it had the advantage of being on the bus route to Birmingham, passing through Sutton, so it suited all of us as far as work was concerned. We moved into 108 in January 1943 and settled down as an ordinary suburban family.

Out of the four of us, there is not much doubt that the greatest effort fell upon mother and my brother Bernard. He was still residing in Hodge Hill Farm and indeed still running the hundred acres of mixed arable and dairy. Unfortunately the tenancy of Hodge Hill Farm was still in father's name and as some of father's creditors had not been paid in full, the Official Receiver (OR) descended on Bernard. He was given the option of continuing to run the farm under the jurisdiction of the OR. The alternative would be to leave the cottage and find other accommodation and also other work. It could also mean potential conscription into the armed forces. As farming was all he knew it really was a 'no brainer' so the option to stay was taken. The terms were he could have £2.10 a week (£2.50 in modern money) whilst any profits would go towards paying father's creditors and no doubt the OR expenses. This was a pittance to keep a wife and two young children. They existed solely because they could virtually live off the farm produce, and I suspect Bernard managed to sell the odd bag of potatoes or some such produce on the side purely to keep their heads above water. This situation continued for some years. His weekly wage was increased eventually to £3.15 (£3.75) but with the end of the war, houses were desperately needed and inroads into Hodge Hill's acres proceeded apace. By 1950 Bernard had no alternative other than to look for other employment.

He was intelligent enough but all he really knew was farming so it was not easy to find new pastures. He eventually settled on the local firm called Mulliners suppliers of metal pressing to the car industry. After a few months on the shop floor he was put in charge of a section. All proceeded smoothly until a dispute occurred between my brother and a worker. An altercation developed and so I understand, the worker told Bernard to "sod off" or words to that effect. Maybe the language was a little more ripe than that but anyway Bernard had been brought up in the school whereby if you fell out with an employee you just sacked him – as simple as that. So he was told to go and collect his cards from the office.

'Tis a pity Bernard had not received any lessons on employer/employee relations since the war! Mulliners was brought to a standstill within 30 minutes. Rapid negotiations took place, the worker was reinstated – Bernard was given a job in the office and peace restored.

Mulliners was eventually taken over, and Bernard moved on to Sheffield Steel in Birmingham. When the Birmingham section was closed down due to reorganisation, Bernard was offered the choice of redundancy or a move to Sheffield. As he was happy in his work and moving to Sheffield did not appeal to Mary or the children, and he did have security of tenure at Hodge Hill Farm cottage, he opted to stay with the Company travelling to Sheffield early on Monday morning and returning on Friday afternoon. He retained residency at the Hodge Hill Farm cottage which he ultimately bought as a sitting tenant. The two children grew up – Derek working all his life for the Accountants Wenham Major, although never qualifying, whilst his sister Stella became a successful hairdresser. Bernard would succumb to cancer in 1996 and died on the 6th May 1997.

Derek still lives in the same farm cottage (now well modernised) whilst Stella married another Bernard who also died of cancer many years ago.

Mother continued working for the Post Office helping to distribute the mail to American forces over here. When that closed down around 1948, she was not so proud and she undertook domestic work for the more well to do in Four Oaks. Mother cycled everywhere and it almost led to tragedy in 1949, she worked for a few hours a week for a family in Somerville Road just over 2 miles from Mere Green and coming home she was knocked off her cycle in Clifton Road and rushed to the Cottage Hospital. Pat was at 108 when a policeman knocked on the door, he was kind enough to say 'not to worry' but mother's had an accident. Pat was taken to the Cottage Hospital to be greeted by a member of staff, who somewhat brusquely told her that she thought Mrs Towers wouldn't last the night. Distraught already this really was not the way to greet a daughter. Pat now rang Mary at Hodge Hill. As it happened, both Bernard and I were at Villa Park where Aston Villa were playing. At some stage I heard an announcement over the loud speaker "would Mr Towers of Hodge Hill report to the Secretary's office". I thought perhaps some cattle had escaped or something of that nature, but after the game I phoned Mary to see if all was OK. Mary was in tears and gave me the news and by now I was in Birmingham outside Snow Hill Station. There was a queue for taxis but very kindly

I was allowed to take the next available cab arriving at the Cottage Hospital around 10 p.m. joining Pat and Bernard and also Pat's great friends Mr and Mrs Allday.

Mother was unconscious – there was nothing we could do other than pray. The Allday's were angels – Pat described them as our second mother and father. They insisted we stay with them for the next few days whilst mother clung on to life, with no sign of regaining consciousness. We took up residence again at 108 after a few days, when we had to go back to work. The nurse who gave mother no more than 24 hours doesn't know the Pywell nature. Many years ago Grandfather Pywell, in his eighties, had been struck down with pneumonia and had been given 48 hours to live. A week later he said he was fed up of lying in bed and got up and fed the chickens. It was two weeks before mother opened her eyes and many more weeks before she came home. She was never the same, with a bit of paralysis of her left side which made her smile a bit lopsided. She never rode her bicycle again; there was an insurance claim eventually. Bernard, as the elder brother, took charge.

He wanted to go to court – mother was adamant she couldn't face it. So agreement was reached in the corridor of the Birmingham Law Court and a figure of £700 was agreed. It meant the mortgage on 108 could be cleared and a bit of cash in the kitty. She didn't work again, but she improved enough to run the home and see Pat and I married. Mother eventually sold 108 and moved to 607 Chester Road, a large terraced house similar to the Mrs Hughes' residence. There she took in lodgers, a Mr and Mrs Galbraith stayed for some years, but the move chiefly was to be nearer her sisters, Auntie Louie at Lytham House and Auntie Cissie just round the corner in Sheffield Road. Mother always said she would never be a burden to her children and years later she took up residence in Icknield House, an old folks residence where she died in July 1977.

Pat meanwhile had been making steady progress in her hairdressing career and having trained at Jayne Bennetts in Birmingham, eventually joined Harry Bryans salon where he traded under the name of "Tudor

Maggie Towers.

Rose". She rapidly built up a successful client base and was a valuable contributor to the family budget.

As I have already mentioned, 108 Mere Green Road was on the bus route to Birmingham, passing through Sutton. The bus stop was 30 yards up the road from 108 and Pat used it on the odd occasion. It didn't take her long to find out that if she came out of the house and turned right, and in a 100 yards turned right into Cremorne Road, she could guarantee one of her boyfriends would stop and give her a lift into Sutton. This was infinitely better than sitting on a crowded bus and also economically advantageous.

Pat and I had learned to hit a tennis ball against the garage door at Home Farm, so it was natural that she would look for a club to join. She was introduced to Streetly Tennis Club where she spent many happy hours particularly at weekends. In those days on a Saturday and Sunday afternoon, when social mixed doubles was the order of the day, the girls sat around waiting to be invited to make up a 'four' as a court became available. From a girls point of view, it was a great advantage if you could hit a decent ball and looked pretty good too. As Pat scored well on both counts, she was kept busy, despite having a non-existent backhand.

However, when it came to finding a long term partner, Pat discarded all the young stags and opted to accept a marriage proposal from Joe Allsop, a successful Sutton butcher who had tragically lost his wife to cancer a couple of years before. She had died leaving Joe with two young children, Joanna who was seven and Guy five. Pat and Joe married in 1951 and whilst they took up residence in Joe's old house, my sister hankered for a fresh start in a new place. She felt there were too many memories in the old house and Joe accepted this, and they soon moved to a large property on the Lichfield Road, close to Four Oaks Station.

Life was not particularly easy for Pat, no problems financially, but it wasn't easy trying to exercise your authority over two step-children, particularly if you were not getting 100% support from your husband. Pat gave up work and they had many happy social occasions. Joe died in 1970, again a cancer victim, and she moved to a flat in Mulroy Road. Pat had taken over a hairdressing business in Lichfield in 1968, in partnership with an old friend Dilys Dyer, and this at least gave her an interest and some independence. Joe had started the Sutton Coldfield Lions Club some years back and through the club she met Sid Harris (a widower) and they married in 1974. Sid was a decorator of some substance (he was a President of the Painters and Decorators Association) and they enjoyed 25 years together until again cancer struck and Sid passed away in 2007.

Pat is now resident in Burcot Court in Four Oaks where she enjoys the best apartment in the block (part of the old school house) and where she will enjoy her 90th birthday in September 2015, and in conjunction with Stella, our niece, who will be celebrating her 70th. Pat still plays a mean game of bridge with a variety of partners (me included), drives her car and lives a hectic social life.

For myself I have already mentioned the Building Society. The thought of four years of studying filled me with dread, so it was with some relief, that I was lucky to walk down Temple Street one day with a lad who worked at Murray & Co. (Stockbrokers). On enquiring where he was off to, I learned he was heading to the offices of *The Birmingham Post and Mail* to see if they had any replies to their advert for an office lad. I enquired more in hope than anything else if they had any exams in the stockbroking profession and was delighted to be informed there were none. I had an interview 48 hours later and started, on what would be my life long profession, a week later.

July 1927 proved to be a wonderful year to be born. It meant I was 18 in July 1945, that being the date I was called up to join the Army. I received my instructions to join His Majesty's Forces in early May, did my six weeks training in N. Ireland and passed out as Private Towers 14059115 in mid-September. As I have pointed out to my 5 children and 16 grandchildren over the years, it cannot be entirely coincidental that Germany surrendered the week I received my calling up papers and the Japanese within a few weeks of finishing my training! I enjoyed a wonderful two and a half years, most of it in Northern Italy starting in Trieste, then Padua and finishing in Venice, where my office was in St. Marc's Square. I spent much of my time playing table tennis and football and dealing with

Peter Towers, aged 19, 1946.

applications for compassionate leave. I did the groundwork and my commanding officer made the decision. When the British forces eventually withdrew from Italy I was lucky enough to be included in the large party of Catholic lads that spent five days in Rome to say goodbye to the Pope. In those five days we had Mass every morning in various famous churches, visit and Mass in the Catacombs, private audience with Pope Pious XII, a breakfast with the Swiss Guards, the Grand Tour of Rome and the icing on the cake coming on the penultimate day with a ticket to attend St. Peter's for the beautification of Maria Goretti where of course the service was carried out by the Pope himself. My abiding memory was the Pope being carried into St. Peter's on his bier and the whole congregation rising to their feet and greeting his Holiness with a roar of "VIVA PAPA" which would have done credit to a football crowd. As a naive young lad I didn't really realise how lucky I was.

On being demobbed in early 1948, I went back to Mere Green Road and Murray & Co. As a young lad I had always been petrified of the dance floor and in my youth club days had always resisted any attempts to get me involved. I had been taking out one Sheila Massey for some time, mainly to the cinema and walks in the park, but she always went dancing on Saturday nights. I decided I had to bite the bullet and booked a course of instruction at the Ninevah dance studio. I made reasonable progress in the waltz, quick step and fox trot, but going round an empty studio is a bit different to navigating one's way round a crowded dance floor. I had resumed my football games with the Abbey FC where we played in the Birmingham Youths & Old Boys league. Two of my team were the Morton brothers and after one Saturday game, I casually asked if anyone had a sister who could dance as I needed a bit of practice. Peter, the elder brother thought his sister, Bernadette, coming up to 17, was unattached and arrangements were completed that the four of us, Peter and Margaret and Bernadette and myself would go to the dance hall in Sutton Park the following Saturday. I was not aware at the time that Bernadette spent almost all her spare time on the dance floor at various dance halls in Birmingham with a variety of partners, all approaching silver or gold medal standard. She must have spent an excruciating evening guiding me around, and glory be she seemed prepared to undergo the same torture the following week. I never did take Sheila out again and Bernadette and I celebrated our Diamond Wedding Anniversary in July 2014. There is a lot to be said for the saying "Tis better to be born lucky than rich".

Over the years Bernadette presented me with two girls, Mandy and Ann, and three boys, Matthew, Richard and Jonathan. They have all been remarkably successful and we are now the proud grandparents of sixteen grandchildren.

Now back to Joseph Austin Towers.

Chapter 23

Early Days Together

Whilst all was turmoil in those later months of 1943 and early 1944, I can be certain of two facts. Prior to his incarceration into Winson Green Prison, my father had regular visits to Vera because somewhere around December 1942 he had once again "hit the jackpot" and made Vera pregnant. Vera subsequently produced a daughter on the 29th August 1943 at Watford Road, Great Barr, Birmingham. Vera had been lodging there but the owners were not keen that Vera should continue her tenancy in the changed circumstances. Joe Towers was not around at this time and whilst I have not been able to confirm the actual date of his prison sentence, it must surely be whilst Vera was giving birth. My father had many faults but the subsequent years would reveal some degree of affection and loyalty to Vera and his daughter Sue.

Faced with eviction and not for the first time, Vera went to see her sister Dolly with baby Sue in her arms. In spite of the fact that Dolly and her "husband" were not married (Dolly and her partner in modern parlance) Vera and Sue were given shelter on the understanding they would have to eat in their own room as she was still, in the Truelove eyes considered to be a "fallen woman".

This situation continued for some months and it has to be assumed that my father came out of prison in the early months of 1944. The visit to my mother at Birmingham Road was, I'm sure, motivated purely and simply by the £100. It was never an attempt to restore the marriage.

It was perfectly natural therefore that he set out to trace Vera's whereabouts and he was soon successful. Vera was at that time living with a Grace and Percy Sawyer. They seemed quite relaxed about the situation and Joe found the odd gardening job to bring in a bit of cash.

Subsequently with a bit of help from the local authority they were rehoused in a small cottage in Lode Lane, Solihull, behind the Olton Hall Public House. So, after nearly 20 years, he found himself back in circumstances very similar to Hodge Hill Farm in 1927. No electricity, no running water and an outside loo!

Next door to the cottage was an extensive army camp with numerous nissen huts of various standards used as accommodation for the soldiers. The Privates got the dregs whilst the higher ranks were established in the higher grade units.

The first ray of sunshine now broke through when my father struck up a friendship with a Sergeant based on the site. They had shared a drink in the Olton Hall Pub and when it became known my father had an agricultural background the Sergeant picked his brains, which solved a problem that had been bugging the Sergeant for some time. When it transpired that there was a problem for the Towers family (Vera was now Mrs Towers with Sue taking the family name) in respect of living accommodation, the Sergeant said he would let my father know when a hut became available. With the war now over and demobilization proceeding apace, it was not long before the family were offered a place. It was, as it had been inferred at the lower end of the scale, but it at least had all mod cons, so that was a step in the right direction. All the lower ranked huts were built as open plan. No permanent divisions, so partitions if needed, were done by curtaining off a portion to provide some privacy. Very much in the style of the old Birmingham "back to backs", mostly now demolished but a few retained for historic purposes and tourist information.

The site was substantial in size with anti-aircraft guns, searchlights and all the requisite buildings for ammunition storage, etc. Joe now set about building up a steady weekly pay packet. He persevered with his gardening activities and also earned the odd pound or so by selling the *Evening Mail* outside the Rover works every evening.

As the buildings became more available the family moved a couple of times in quick succession, and with the farming life still coursing through his veins, it wasn't long before he took possession of an unused hut, cleaned it out and back we go to chicken farming. No need now to be worried about being caught in a compromising situation. As he was now approaching 60 and was physically working harder than he had for many years, I suspect his libido was on the wane and anyway Vera was now more available than in the past.

He now had a new line of income, albeit very modest, with the sale of hens eggs. By good luck and one cannot in all reality begrudge that minor change in his fortune, in spite of the fact he brought most of the disasters on himself, a piece of land on the opposite side of Lode Lane was derelict. Council owned, he asked the authorities of he could use it, and was granted permission on the understanding that it would be needed for redevelopment in due course and his notice to quit would be very short.

On this basis, the chicken business took a surge. A couple of cockerels were bought and fertilised eggs were hatched. The chicks were added to the flock and what was a mere side line became a decent income producer.

However there was one problem, namely little Sue. She loved helping to look after the chickens, feeding and collecting the eggs. But as she sailed past her 4th birthday and rapidly approached school age, Vera was happy and expected no more than a Council school education. Joe had more ambitious ideas. His first family had all received a private education and he saw no reason why Sue should be any different. All well and good if the annual income is sufficient to meet the bills, but the chicken farm plus part-time gardening didn't really put him in that bracket. The problem seemed insurmountable and, foreign to his nature he decided to bite the bullet and go cap in hand to his father. Grandfather Towers had retired and left the Midlands to spend his remaining years in Torquay. The rest of the family kept in touch and from his sister, Muriel he obtained Grandfather's address. He thought it best to keep his visit a surprise in the fond hope that the unexpected visit may be more fruitful.

The unexpected at least worked and he was shown up to his father's room at the Hotel where he was staying. After the usual pleasantries, which at least got the meeting off to a reasonable start, my father must have put his case like an expert barrister. The decision was that no way was he going to be reinstated into Grandfather's will, and purely as a one off he was given a life policy and told he could encash that for what he could get and that would be the end of the matter. It turned out that the gesture was quite generous and the policy produced a few hundred pounds.

Sue was now in a position to proceed with a private education and eventually she was enrolled in Ruckleigh School (opposite Solihull Hospital) and started her education in September 1948 at the tender age of 5 and a bit. Sue took to school straight away, the only problem was her living accommodation. All the other pupils came from an entirely different background and it was deemed advisable to reject invitations to parties as such on the realisation that there was a substantial difference in life styles.

Chapter 24

Glimmer of Light

With Sue now at school her father renewed his efforts to expand the Poultry business. The chicken side now included a few geese and turkeys for the Christmas market. The geese were excellent watchdogs and Joe solved the local fox problem by sitting up until the early hours with his 12 bore shot gun.

This side of the business was now producing a steady income with the sale of eggs on a door to door basis. The Christmas trade with by now 30 geese and 50 turkeys (to go with 500 chickens) was a bonus and with the odd gardening job and selling the *Evening Mail* at the Rover works, life took on a rosier hue than for many moons. He was troubled occasionally by a claim from mother for some financial support, but even pursued through the courts, it produced a plea of poverty and perhaps the odd postal order of 5 or 10 shillings (25p or 50p in modern terms). I can't say it altered our life style.

Life continued on a fairly even keel for the next year or so. Vera had learned over the years to mind her P's and Q's. While Bernard, Tom and I had felt the weight of father's hand on more than one occasion, he had never raised his hand to Pat. It seems Vera was also privy to this exclusion, but Sue for some reason was not exempt from the odd bit of corporal punishment. On the other side of the coin he could be generous. When Sue was eight, she came home from school one early

Joe's poultry venture, early 1950s.

Joe displaying one of his turkeys, early 1950s.

spring day to find she had a present in the shape of two young lambs. As a young girl, you can't get a much better present. They were rapidly christened as Button and Bows. They were Sue's to feed on the bottle until they were able to graze, but inevitably as they grew they were passed on to a local farmer.

During the period they had been living on the Army site, there had been a number of opportunities for the family to move to a slightly better building. With the end of the War in 1945 and demobilisation gathering pace it was only natural that this should happen. The result after a couple of moves saw them now installed in officer's quarters, which was a substantial improvement on the first building offered to them.

Vera now found she had time on her hands, and in the immediate post war years, it was not difficult to find a job. A local shop specialising in bread, cakes and such delicacies as could be produced at that time needed a part-time worker and as it was within walking distance, Vera applied and was taken on. She took to the job like a duck to water and this was the catalyst for a review of the family situation. Within 12 months, Vera was being pressured to work full-time with an attractive salary to go with it. It was agreed that Joe would ease up on his gardening activities so he was at home mid-afternoon for Sue's return from school.

This system worked well for a year of so with Vera ending up as a Manageress of the shop. Joe's progress on the domestic front was equally impressive and his ability in the kitchen, not only to produce afternoon tea, but subsequently to cook a full blown dinner, would have left my mother open mouthed in amazement. I am led to believe his steak and kidney pie became quite a delicacy.

Throughout Sue's growing years, neither Sue nor her father had ever set foot in a Catholic Church. No great surprise here for he had certainly broken one or two of the Church's Commandments – the one about adultery springs to mind.

It seems though, that in some cases, and this appears to have applied to my father, once the seed of Catholicism has been planted in the early

Feeding the poultry, early 1950s.

Feeding the poultry, early 1950s.

days, it can come to life in later years. Sue had done extremely well at junior school and thoughts were turning to her senior school. Continuing the policy of private education for all his off-springs, Joe fixed an appointment to see the Reverend Mother of the Convent School attached to St Bernard's Oratory in Solihull. He must have kissed the Blarney Stone before the interview because a place would be available if certain conditions were met. First she must pass the entrance examination and secondly she must study the faith to prepare for the three sacraments of Confession, Holy Communion and Confirmation. So Sue's scholastic future, assuming she could pass the exam, was writ in stone.

Chapter 25

Consolidation

However, before we reach Sue's 11th birthday, a few more changes took place in respect of the family's accommodation. I have already mentioned the moves into better buildings with superior facilities, which obviously improved their way of life. As the end of the 1940s approached, the site was being vacated more rapidly, month by month, with inevitable consequences. In late 1949, Joe received the long awaited notice to quit. With no capital reserves (at least none that he was going to reveal to the Council – at least on this occasion the official receiver was not breathing down his neck) he approached the Council. Pleading his case he had nowhere to go, they were subsequently rehoused in a prefab in early 1950. Prefabs (prefabricated buildings) were designed to solve or at least help to rehouse those who had lost their homes through bombing in the war. They could be erected in a matter of days and were meant to be a short term solution. Many of them were still in use at the turn of the century and were much loved by their tenant.

With the move from the Army site, it inevitably saw the end of the poultry venture. The prefab they took possession of was situated in Lode Lane opposite Olton Hall Pub. Vera had found her true vocation and was now manageress of her shop and was earning a reasonable salary. Joe now became the housekeeper. That was all well and good but the family were hardly wallowing in cash. Anyway Joe wasn't so old that he couldn't turn his hand to something. The solution came when he spotted an advert in *The Birmingham Evening Mail* for a night watchman's job at a local factory with hours 8 p.m. to 6 a.m. A long stint but hardly taxing from a vigorous point of view. The night could be passed by listening to the radio and the mandatory walk around the premises to ensure all was in order. Prior to accepting the job he had spent what capital he had saved and raised from the poultry sales on the acquisition of a small car. This enabled him to go to his night job with his 12 bore shot gun in the boot. On his night time patrol round the factory, he now felt he was reasonably secure should he meet any intruders.

Life became even better when Vera was "head-hunted". I doubt that phrase had been used in the early 1950s, but she was persuaded to join Wimbush, a much larger retailer. It wasn't long before she was promoted to run both the Solihull shops. Again an increase in wages and with Joe bringing in a reasonable salary, things were looking much brighter.

Outside the economic environment, the outlook for Vera and Sue was also greatly improved. Turning the clock back to Hodge Hill Farm in the 1930s and Home Farm in the period 1936/42, my father was very rarely at home in the evenings. Now with Vera and Sue he hardly ever went out which was a total reversal of earlier behaviour. They were not the happiest of times as far as Sue and Vera were concerned. Joe still ruled the roost and could be a bit of a tyrant. However, with the advent of the night watchman's job and also the retention of the newspaper sales at the Rover works, Vera and Sue could now enjoy the evenings at home by themselves.

An interesting note is the fact that until the day he died, my father refused to recognise the switch to the decimal currency and always in his own mind worked in pounds, shillings and pence. Just another indication of the stubborn streak that dominated his life.

Chapter 26

A Working Family

In 1954 Sue sailed through her entrance exam for the Olton Court Convent School in Saint Bernard's Road, Olton, and once again the process of fitting her out with all the appropriate clothing had to be pursued. This was the least of Sue's problems. She was naturally shy and, as at junior school, there was a substantial difference in social class with the vast majority of the other girls. This certainly did not affect Sue's academic ability and she sailed through her school career with considerable success. As promised, she also completed the obligations of making her first confession, holy communion and confirmation, without ever becoming a devoted Catholic. But then my father I suspect was never a shining role model in this respect.

However, in spite of doing well academically, Sue had no intention of prolonging her days at school a day longer than necessary. As at junior school, the difference in social class purely from the living accommodation point of view, made close friendships difficult. This still applied at senior school and anyway, Sue, with her mother's help had no difficulty in obtaining a Saturday job at the local Wimbush shop. This ensured she was not available to meet classmates on Saturday mornings in Solihull centre and the absence of close friends was no real hardship. The bit of money also gave her a feeling of independence. So, after a couple of years or so, at the end of the summer term in 1958, agreement was reached in the family that Sue would not return in September for the following year. In monetary terms this put the family in a more healthy financial position. No more school fees, and Wimbush greeted Sue with open arms as she happily accepted full time employment.

The next two years saw a consolidation in the family life style. Both Vera and Sue saw promotion, with Sue consistently the most successful sales girl in her branch. She was helped in this respect by using her father as an assistant. He would take some of the cakes and nicknacks provided by Sue to his paper stand in the evening. The workers from the Rover factory were happy enough to pick up a couple of delicacies to cheer up the little lady at home.

Domestic life now became quite settled although both Vera and Sue needed to watch their P's and Q's. Sue had grown into a very attractive young lady and Vera, in spite of the passing years still had a trim figure. Sue introduced the occasional young man into the household but they were invariably given short shrift by her father. If they couldn't converse in agricultural terms they were not encouraged to return. He also kept a close watch on Vera, and when one evening she was injudicious enough to let a male colleague from Wimbush give her a lift home, the balloon went up. Father threatened all sorts of reprisals if it happened again, and Vera was wise enough to make sure it didn't. In the light of his past behaviour, a classic example of "do what I say not what I do".

Joe Towers was now approaching his 70th birthday and his health had been deteriorating for some months. At the same time, Sue hit her 17th birthday and it had been agreed that she could start to learn to drive. The usual preliminaries were gone through and a provisional licence obtained. During that Autumn of 1960 Sue made good progress, and with 3 or 4 lessons from a professional instructor Sue took her first test. All seemed to go well but the dreaded "failed" ticket was produced. The reason given "over confidence". The second test a few weeks later saw a more subdued pupil approach everything a little more cautiously, and this time the "passed" ticket was produced.

Whilst her father had consistently persevered with Sue's driving lessons, his health was deteriorating quite remarkably. His appetite had virtually disappeared and he was surviving on cherry cake, tea and little else. He was down from a normal 11/12 stone to 9 stone and was finding it impossible to stand up straight. His condition was obviously causing both Vera and Sue a great deal of concern and in that late Autumn/early Winter of 1960, the family were fortunate to spot an advert for a health clinic.

This was in Weymouth, so enquiries were made, costs ascertained, and between them Vera and Sue financed a two week stay in the optimistic hope that it would prove beneficial. Not yet having driven anywhere outside of Solihull since she passed her test, Sue now undertook the somewhat hazardous journey to Weymouth and back. No 'satnav' in those days although virtually all the signposts, which had disappeared during the war, were now back in place. With copious maps and directions and father's navigational skills such as they were, the destination was arrived at. Father was installed and Sue drove safely back to Solihull the same day, no small feat for an inexperienced driver. It is perhaps worth noting that Joe's absence for those two weeks turned out to be a virtual holiday for Vera and Sue, freed from the dictatorial atmosphere they usually lived under.

It is probably true to say that those 14 days passed all too quickly, but from the telephone conversations it seemed that Joe was making progress. When Sue eventually undertook the return journey to Weymouth and she first saw her father she couldn't believe the transformation. He was standing up straight, was well on the way to regaining his weight and looking tanned. Pernicious anaemia had been diagnosed and a diet of molasses and various health foods appeared to have done the trick.

Chapter 27

Romance and a New Home

On his return from Weymouth, Joe resumed night watchman's duties which were not unduly onerous, whilst Vera and Sue continued with their Wimbush careers. Whilst this record is mainly about my father it is only right that the contribution made by Vera and Sue to the financial well-being of the family is recognised.

Sue had been working full-time since leaving school and in the early months of 1960, she had been moved to the Knowle Branch as Manageress at the tender age of sixteen and a half, a record that has probably never been equalled in the retail trade.

Previously, Vera had been Manageress of both the Knowle and Solihull shops, but the company had plans for greater things for the Towers family. Over the next 2/3 years, they both obviously continued to impress the Wimbush management to the extent that in 1963 they were both promoted to the role of Supervisors. Vera would be in charge of some 10 shops in the central Birmingham area, whilst Sue was to be responsible for the outlying areas stretching as far as Hereford and Worcestershire. No problems for Sue as she was now an experienced driver and a company vehicle was provided. Vera's promotion however was contingent on her learning to drive. Lessons were hastily organised but the promotion had to be deferred as Vera struggled to pass her driving test. At the fourth time of asking, the 'pass' ticket was produced, and Vera was installed as Supervisor. Whilst the family did not exactly become a three vehicle owning household, they certainly had access to that number. The family income was now sufficient for savings to start accumulating.

Family life continued in a fairly normal fashion with the exception that Vera became virtually housebound in the evenings. Joe was extremely jealous and Vera took the view that as she quite enjoyed a quiet life at home, it was not worth the hassle to go against his wishes. Meanwhile there were no such restrictions placed on Sue, and anyway she was now a grown up independent woman and, as such, one of her social activities was an evening dancing at the 'Galleon' on the Stratford Road. It was here one Saturday night in 1965 that cupid's arrow hit home. One David Field had been (excuse the pun) eying the field and plucked up the courage to ask Sue for a dance. If it wasn't earth shattering on that first night, it certainly developed into a romance that many couples hope for but few attain. Fortunately the major hurdle was surmounted without any difficulty. His introduction to Sue's father went off without a hitch. David was a good listener and genuinely interested in his farming background. The courtship developed over the next year or so with both Joe and Vera becoming more and more convinced that Sue had found the ideal potential husband. This proved to be the case and David duly, having ascertained that Sue would say yes when he went down on one knee and popped the question, in the old fashioned time honoured way asked Joe if he could propose to Sue. The answer of course was in the affirmative.

While they had resided in the Prefab for some years, Joe had badgered the Council on a number of occasions for a move into better accommodation and this had borne fruit in 1964 when the family moved to a semi-detached house in Windrush Close in the Hobs Moat area of Solihull. This was a distinct move up in the social order of things and they celebrated by having new carpets throughout and Vera's pride and joy was the new red velvet curtains in the lounge. Sue chipped in by buying her mother a new china tea service.

Chapter 28

New Home No.2

Early in 1968 Sue and David, now that the wedding date was fixed for October, began house hunting. In those days the size of mortgage a couple could obtain relied on the man's income only. Fortunately David's salary was above average and with Sue's earnings in reserve they were in a reasonably strong position. After inspecting a number of houses they settled on a place in Hollywood Lane in Hollywood, a suburb of Birmingham. Contracts were exchanged and on the 1st April 1968 they took possession of a semi-detached, three bedroomed property with garage attached. It needed a bit of work, and David and Sue spent the summer months licking the place into shape. On the 12th October on returning from honeymoon they took up residence in their new home. One snag.

The journey to where Joe and Vera lived was the best part of half an hour if the traffic was bad, which was often. Many newlyweds would consider this a blessing in disguise but not in this particular case. The purchase of the house almost fell through in the early part of the negotiations as the property had a very substantial rear garden which ran all the way down to Mayhurst Road. The owner had run a bit of a market garden but the bottom half was not included in the original contract. The seller wanted an extra £100 for the full site, but Sue and David had put all their reserves into the deposit. Fortunately Joe and

Vera felt it would be a good investment and came up with the £100 to seal the contract.

Once again, we have the slightly strange situation whereby, in spite of being a luke-warm Catholic in his own life, Joe was insistent that Sue and David must have a Catholic Wedding. This carried the complication that David as a non-Catholic was obliged to take certain instructions as to his obligations in a 'mixed' marriage. They were not unduly onerous, the main one being that any children should be brought up in the Catholic Faith. As Sue had connections with the Friary during her school days, David had his instruction from Father Thomas Moore who was based there. They hit it off very well together, David being particularly impressed and it was agreed Father Tom would conduct the ceremony. Originally the wedding was booked to take place at the Friary but a mix up over the dates necessitated a move to Our Lady of the Wayside where the Parish Priest was quite happy to step to one side and let Father Tom tie the knot as it were.

The 5th October 1968 was a bright autumn day as her father escorted Sue down the aisle. I suspect he felt a particular sense of pride as he had missed out on Pat's celebrations. He had, of course, attended Bernard's wedding many years earlier but he also missed mine in 1954. However boys weddings don't really compare with giving your daughter away.

After the ceremony a group of around thirty retired to the George Hotel in Solihull to enjoy the festivities. The gathering consisted almost entirely of David's relations – he had three sisters – and no mention was ever made of Joe's previous family, the secret being jealously guarded. Sue and David had a one week honeymoon in Torquay returning on the 12th October. Sue resumed work at Wimbush whilst David, who was a qualified electrician returned to work with a colleague in the private sector. David had been invited to join in a partnership but was somewhat apprehensive about sacrificing a fixed salary against a share of unknown profits. He subsequently moved on to other employment with more established companies, finally ending up with Vodafone where he did modestly well when they were privatised.

Sue's Wedding, 5 October, 1968.

Sue and father, 1968.

Above: Sue's wedding with her father and bridesmaids.

Left: Sue's Wedding with David, Sue, Joe and Vera.

Chapter 29

Grandad Again

The next couple of years passed with not much to report. Vera continued working at Wimbush but Joe had by now retired. As Vera had company transport, he had parted with his car which was another cash saving move. He spent some of his spare time at Sue and David's place by bringing his agricultural experience into play, and licking the substantial garden into shape. It was a bit like turning the clock back to the early days of the second World War, when the Farm Shop was opened at Hodge Hill Farm.

It was not difficult to sell the surplus produce, the proceeds from which he was quite prepared to hand over to Sue. A far cry from the years at Home Farm when to get money from him in those days was like the proverbial "getting blood out of a stone".

1970 was uneventful, not that Sue, or David for that matter, would subscribe to that view. In fact it turned out to be a wonderful year as Sue became pregnant. I could be using a bit of poetic licence here as I suppose the seed could have been sown in early '71. Anyway, whether it was Christmas celebrations in 1970 or New Year high jinks in 1971, the result was a daughter Jo arriving in September 1971.

All went well, although obviously Sue had given up work some three months earlier. She had no intention of going back to work as Sue considered being a mother was a full time occupation. Not a view shared by many professional working young mums in this day and age, but times and views change as the years tick on.

On the other hand with the loss of Sue's salary, and she had been over the years a bigger contributor to the family budget, money was going to be a bit tight. Sue therefore launched on a part time career selling Tupperware, Avon and other products by the process of holding "house parties".

David had by now acquired his own car which was a blessing as Sue no longer had the luxury of a company vehicle.

1972 and early 1973 followed a quiet pattern before 1974 arrived to test the durability of the family. It all started with Sue finding herself pregnant again in early 1973. All went well for the first month or so and all the family were absolutely delighted when twins were diagnosed. Things deteriorated as Autumn approached and Sue went into hospital late September where she would remain until January 1974, when she safely produced twin girls.

Although the new arrivals were sound in wind and limb, when Sue arrived home it coincided with Vera having a spell in hospital with ulcer problems, and ultimately a hysterectomy. With Joe now 85 and showing his age, there was not a great deal of help coming from her parents. Indeed, in those early days it was all a bit of a nightmare. With only one car, Sue was up early with 3 children in the back of the car, she took David to work. Back home to lick things into shape and then a 20/30 minute drive to look after her mother and father.

It didn't take long for Sue and David to decide things couldn't go on as they were. It was David's insistence that the only solution was for Joe and Vera to come and live with them. I venture to suggest there are not many son-in-laws who would take such a view and it is a measure of his character that he did so.

They gave up their own bedroom to her mother and father and moved into bedroom no. 2 themselves, whilst Jo, now 3, had the third bedroom. The twins slept in the lounge!

Over the next month or so, Vera was restored to full health and returned to work at Wimbush. It was decided that David would build a bedroom over the garage and their parents move would be permanent. The tenancy of Windrush Close was closed and David set about the building project. He did the entire job himself often working until the early hours. Father was able to do the odd labouring job moving materials, etc. and later that year the family were in a position where everyone could sleep upstairs.

Vera now made the decision to work part time. The company agreed that she could do her supervisory job whilst working mornings only and this proved to be a great help.

Joe Towers' health continued to deteriorate and in late January 1976, he went into East Birmingham Hospital where he passed away on 2nd February 1976. The cause of death was given as "Congestive Heart Failure and Coronary Thrombosis". Sue and David would go on to build another house at the bottom of the garden fronting on to Mayhurst Road. Designed and built again by David but with some help with the plastering and roofing work. They moved into the new property in the late 1970s and Vera had her own lounge if needs be. Sue would return to work, not at Wimbush, which had now merged and become "Three Cooks", but at Sainsburys starting at the bottom as a shelf stacker. She would work there for 25 years moving up the ladder and ultimately finishing in Management training. Her career there almost floundered when she opted out of a meeting with senior executives due to her shyness and perhaps lack of confidence. She was told in no uncertain terms that should she do that again, she would be looking for a new job. Vera continued to work for Wimbush and retired in 1983 when the company merged with "Three Cooks".

Chapter 30

Epilogue

With my father dying in 1976 and mother passing away in 1977 the story of Joe and Maggie Towers' life together and eventually apart came to an end. Most families will have a similar tale to relate but perhaps mother and father's is slightly above average.

There was a sequel many years later which I think is worth putting on record. As the 20th century drew to a close I had been toying with the idea of putting pen to paper and placing on record these details for the benefit of the children and grandchildren. With Bernard being struck down with cancer and with his knowledge of the early days at Langley Mill and Hodge Hill it became imperative I picked his brains. I was a bit apprehensive about asking him as the implication was fairly obvious, if we don't do it soon, the opportunity may disappear. In his usual phlegmatic manner he said he would be delighted and in the latter part of 1996 – I never recorded the actual date – I took my tape recorder to Hodge Hill Farm (now re-designated as 150 Hodge Hill Road, Ward End) he poured out memories for the best part of three hours and at the end confirmed he felt absolutely shattered.

That really would have been the end of the story except for the fact that my curiosity got the better of me and I felt I wanted to know more about my father's later life. Knowing some sketchy details about Vera working for "Three Cooks" and taking the view "nothing ventured, nothing gained" I phoned Head Office. Upon my request to speak to someone in the Personnel Department, I found myself speaking to Carol. I asked if by any chance she knew a Vera Truelove or a Vera Towers and was delighted to learn that "yes of course" was the reply.

"Are you still in touch?" I enquired and again it was good news. Carol and Vera exchanged Christmas cards and had the occasional chat over the phone. "Could you possibly give me her phone number or address?" drew the diplomatic reply "What's it about?" "It's a personal matter" and this was followed by Carol taking a very sensible decision that she felt she couldn't do that, but give me your name and I will phone Vera and tell her you are trying to get in touch.

I left my name and telephone number with her and let nature take its course. I didn't really know whether I expected a reply or not. When it came I was to a certain extent devastated, as it appeared I had stirred up a hornets nest.

Carol had phoned Vera the following day but unknown to me, Vera was now living with Sue and David. When the phone rang, naturally Sue who was upstairs answered. As Sue, who also knew Carol very well, had a little chat and exchanged the usual pleasantries, Carol then asked could she speak to Vera. Sue shouts down "Mom, Carol's on the phone, would you like a word?", and when Vera answered, puts her phone down. The news that a Peter Towers was trying to get in touch was absolutely devastating. After a mumbled response Vera put the phone down. A few moments later Sue breezes into the lounge and says, "What did Carol want? Good God Mom, what's happened? You've gone as white as a sheet."

"No, no it's nothing."

"Mom, don't be silly, has someone died?"

"No, no really it's nothing." Sue is now like a dog with a bone and is not going to give up. After gentle persuasion and many tears, Vera eventually produces the phrase "Your Dad made me promise never to tell you." If Sue had been prepared to let go of the bone, there was now not the slightest chance.

Sue's nature and her obvious love for her Mom and Dad meant that this was a battle Vera was never going to win and so the whole story was poured out. Sue was traumatized. She had always wondered about the age gap, the absence of wedding photos, no relatives on either side and no real early history.

It was perhaps about a week before the phone rang at home and I found myself speaking to a David Field who patiently explained what had happened. He said this had come as an enormous shock and could he possibly come over by himself just to meet us. Bernadette and I of course agreed and a couple of days later this well-built slightly bearded chap presented himself. We talked for an hour or so and it seems we came across as a fairly normal couple. If we didn't score 10/10, the rating was high enough for David to ring us the following day and say that Sue would like a word.

That phone call was one of those joyful occasions that don't happen all that often. Sue was crying saying she had always wanted a family and regretted for so long that she was an only child. A date was fixed for the following week and David and Sue came over one evening and had dinner with us. I doubt that, had we been able to choose out of half the population, we could have done any better than this couple to enlarge our family.

Over the next few months they met all the family and Sue visited Bernard many, many times as the cancer took a firmer grip and he neared his end. For the best part of the last two decades we have shared Wedding Anniversaries, special birthdays, weddings of their three girls, met David's family and shared Sue's sorrow as David succumbed to cancer in 2013.

I called on Sue one afternoon when I happened to be on their side of Birmingham to find Vera answering the door. Sue had gone for a walk and would be back in half an hour or so. We sat in Vera's own lounge and chatted until Sue returned. We had obviously met Vera previously and Sue had told me that her mother still found it difficult to talk about her earlier years, so I was reluctant to press too hard. It would have been nice to have had a session, such as that which I had with Bernard, to put on record some of her experiences with my father over the years. However diplomacy, which is not usually my strong point, prevailed and sleeping dogs were left to lie. Sue was able to provide me with all the facts of Dad's later life.